DECONSTRUCTING NORMATIVITY?

Deconstructing Normativity? brings together a unique collection of chapters in which an international selection of contributors reflect on the fundamental and often very radical ideas present in Freud's original 1905 edition of the *Three Essays on the Theory of Sexuality*.

The book has three aims: the contextualization of the text, the reconstruction of its central ideas and the further philosophical reflection of the contemporary relevance and critical potential of the 1905 edition. The authors challenge mainstream interpretations of the *Three Essays*, generally based on readings of the final 1924 edition of the text, and of the development of Freudian thought: including, most importantly, the centrality of the Oedipus complex and the developmental approach relative to a tendency towards heteronormativity. *Deconstructing Normativity?* makes an important contribution in rethinking Freudian psychoanalysis and reopening the discussion on its central paradigms, and in so doing it connects with queer and gender theories and philosophical approaches.

This book will be essential reading for psychoanalysts in practice and training, as well as academics and students of psychoanalysis, philosophical anthropology, continental philosophy, sex, gender and sexualities.

Philippe Van Haute is professor of philosophical anthropology at Radboud University, the Netherlands, and extraordinary professor at the University of Pretoria, South Africa. He is a practising psychoanalyst and was president of the Belgian School for Psychoanalysis from 2006 to 2009.

Herman Westerink is lecturer at the Center for Contemporary European Philosophy, Radboud University, the Netherlands, and extraordinary professor at the Catholic University of Leuven, Belgium.

DECONSTRUCTING NORMATIVITY?

Re-reading Freud's 1905
Three Essays

*Edited by Philippe Van Haute
and Herman Westerink*

LONDON AND NEW YORK

First published 2017
by Routledge
2 Park Square, Milton Park, Abingdon, Oxon OX14 4RN

and by Routledge
711 Third Avenue, New York, NY 10017

Routledge is an imprint of the Taylor & Francis Group, an informa business

© 2017 selection and editorial matter, P. Van Haute and H. Westerink; individual chapters, the contributors

The right of the editors to be identified as the authors of the editorial material, and of the authors for their individual chapters, has been asserted in accordance with sections 77 and 78 of the Copyright, Designs and Patents Act 1988.

All rights reserved. No part of this book may be reprinted or reproduced or utilised in any form or by any electronic, mechanical, or other means, now known or hereafter invented, including photocopying and recording, or in any information storage or retrieval system, without permission in writing from the publishers.

Trademark notice: Product or corporate names may be trademarks or registered trademarks, and are used only for identification and explanation without intent to infringe.

British Library Cataloguing-in-Publication Data
A catalogue record for this book is available from the British Library

Library of Congress Cataloging-in-Publication Data
Names: Van Haute, Philippe, 1957 – editor. | Westerink, Herman, 1968 – editor.
Title: Deconstructing normativity?: re-reading Freud's 1905 three essays / edited by Philippe Van Haute and Herman Westerink.
Description: Abingdon, UK; New York: Routledge, 2017. | Includes bibliographical references.
Identifiers: LCCN 2016037039 | ISBN 9781138232570 (hbk.: alk. paper) | ISBN 9781138232594 (pbk.: alk. paper) | ISBN 9781315312255 (ebk)
Subjects: | MESH: Freud, Sigmund, 1856–1939. Drei Abhandlungen zur Sexualtheorie. | Sexual Behavior—psychology | Sexuality—psychology | Freudian Theory | Psychoanalytic Interpretation
Classification: LCC RC509 | NLM WM 460.5.S3 | DDC 616.89/17—dc23
LC record available at https://lccn.loc.gov/2016037039

ISBN: 978-1-138-23257-0 (hbk)
ISBN: 978-1-138-23259-4 (pbk)
ISBN: 978-1-315-31225-5 (ebk)

Typeset in Bembo
by Swales & Willis, Exeter, Devon, UK

CONTENTS

Contributors   vii

Introduction: excavating a theory of sexuality   1
Philippe Van Haute and Herman Westerink

1   Understanding Freud's conflicted view of the object-relatedness of sexuality and its implications for contemporary psychoanalysis: a re-examination of *Three Essays on the Theory of Sexuality*   6
Rachel Blass

2   Freud's discussion with psychiatry on sexuality, drives and objects in *Three Essays*   28
Herman Westerink

3   The pre-Freudian modernization of sexuality: Richard von Krafft-Ebing and Albert Moll   44
Harry Oosterhuis

4   The mystery of the erased sentence in Freud's *Three Essays on the Theory of Sexuality*   55
Patrick Vandermeersch

5   Freud reads Krafft-Ebing: the case of sadism and masochism   64
Jens De Vleminck

6 Variations, components and accidents: critical reflections
   on Freud's concept of the drive   87
   Monique David-Ménard

7 Lacan meets Freud? Patho-analytic reflections on the status
   of the perversions in Lacanian metapsychology   101
   Philippe Van Haute

   Epilogue: the *Three Essays* today   116
   Philippe Van Haute and Herman Westerink

Index   120

CONTRIBUTORS

Rachel Blass is a member and training analyst at the Israel Psychoanalytic Society, a member of the British Psychoanalytical Society, professor of psychoanalysis at Heythrop College, and visiting professor at UCL, University of London. She is also a board member and editor of the 'Controversies' section of the *International Journal of Psychoanalysis*. She recently published amongst others 'Further evidence for the case against neuropsychoanalysis: How Yovell, Solms, and Fotopoulou's response to our critique confirms the irrelevance and harmfulness to psychoanalysis of the contemporary neuroscientific trend', in *International Journal of Psychoanalysis* (with Z. Carmelli, 2015) and 'The quest for truth as the foundation of psychoanalytic practice: A traditional, Freudian-Kleinian perspective', in *The Psychoanalytic Quarterly* (2016).

Monique David-Ménard is professor emeritus of philosophy at the Centre d'études du vivant, Université Paris-Diderot, and practising psychoanalyst in Paris (Société de Psychanalyse Freudienne). She is a cofounder of the International Society for Psychanalysis and Philosophy (ISPP/SIPP) and member of the International Network of Women Philosophers at UNESCO. Recent publications include 'Objects, exchanges, discourse' (Scholarly dialogue on psychoanalysis and philosophy in the work of Monique David-Ménard) in *philoSOPHIA: A Journal of Continental Feminism* (2015).

Philippe Van Haute is professor of philosophical anthropology at Radboud University, the Netherlands and extraordinary professor at the University of Pretoria, South Africa. He is a practising psychoanalyst and he was president of the Belgian School for Psychoanalysis from 2006 to 2009. He recently published (with Tomas Geyskens) *Towards a Non-Oedipal Psychoanalysis? Clinical Anthropology in Freud and Lacan* (2012) and he edited with Ulrike Kistner and Herman Westerink the 1905 edition of Freud's *Three Essays on the Theory of Sexuality* (2016).

Jens De Vleminck is philosopher, sexologist and psychoanalyst. He is a postdoctoral fellow in philosophy at Ghent University, Belgium, and secretary of the Belgian School for Psychoanalysis (École Belge de Psychanalyse). He is co-editor of *Sexuality and Psychoanalysis: Philosophical Criticisms* (2010). Forthcoming amongst others 'La pulsion de mort chez Freud. L'Evolution Psychiatrique' (2016).

Harry Oosterhuis teaches history at the Faculty of Arts and Social Sciences of Maastricht University and he is affiliated to the Huizinga Research School for Cultural History in Amsterdam. His research focuses on the cultural and social history of psychiatry and mental health care, of sexuality and gender, of health and citizenship and of bicycling. He is author of *Stepchildren of Nature: Krafft-Ebing, Psychiatry, and the Making of Sexual Identity* (2000), and co-editor of *Psychiatric Cultures Compared. Psychiatry and Mental Health Care in the Twentieth Century: Comparisons and Approaches* (2005).

Patrick Vandermeersch studied philosophy and theology and was trained as a psychoanalyst. He was professor of ethics and the history of sexuality at the Catholic University of Leuven, Belgium (1978–1992), and full professor of psychology of religion at the Faculty of Theology and Religious Studies of the University of Groningen, the Netherlands (1992–2008). His most important books include *Unresolved Questions in the Freud/Jung Debate: On Psychosis, Sexual Identity and Religion* (1991) and *La chair de la Passion. Une histoire de foi: la flagellation* (2002).

Herman Westerink is lecturer at the Center for Contemporary European Philosophy, Radboud University Nijmegen, the Netherlands, and extraordinary professor at the Catholic University of Leuven, Belgium. His publications in the field of psychoanalysis, psychology and philosophy of religion include *A Dark Trace: Sigmund Freud on the Sense of Guilt* (2009) and *The Heart of Man's Destiny* (2012). He is editor of the book series *Sigmund Freuds Werke: Wiener Interdiszipliäre Kommentare*.

INTRODUCTION

Excavating a theory of sexuality

Philippe Van Haute and Herman Westerink

There is no doubt that the *Three Essays on the Theory of Sexuality* is one of Freud's most important and original writings. It can be seen as the culmination and the almost inevitable outcome of the intuitions and thoughts that are found in his earliest psychoanalytic writings from the 1890s. After all, in the aetiology of the psychoneuroses the sexual factor is the decisive one, and this calls for theoretical inquiry into the very nature of sexuality. For this inquiry and the subsequent theory, Freud not only builds his arguments on his own clinical findings but also turns his attention to the findings of the psychiatrists and sexologists of his time. And for this very reason, the text connects to a whole body of literature. Nevertheless, the *Three Essays* is anything but inevitable and is by no means the continuation of a body and style of thought. Already in the first paragraphs of the text, Freud radically distances himself from the 'popular opinions' and 'poetic fables' which he claims characterize the contemporary scientific literature on the relation between sexuality and its perverse aberrations. Freud turns the general reasoning of this literature upside down by taking his starting point in the perversions – the polymorphous perverse nature of the sexual drive – in order to conceptualize normal sexuality. And since Freud systematically adopts the psychiatric and sexological conceptual framework for the first time in 1905, the *Three Essays* also cannot just be read as the more or less systematic assemblage of previously developed clinical insights and thoughts on sexuality and its significance in the aetiology of the psychoneuroses. The *Three Essays* is both the outcome of these insights and thoughts, and their fundamental revision in the light of a new conceptual framework.

So, what exactly are these original elements, inevitable developments and revised conceptions wherein lies the continuity with Freud's previous writings and those of his predecessors? What can we identify as radically new, or as the major theoretical and methodological innovations and shifts? Decisive for any answer to such questions is a more basic question: Which text do we read? We know that

Freud published the *Three Essays* in 1905, and then reissued the text in 1910, 1915, 1920 and 1924, each time inserting additional elements containing new theoretical material that fundamentally disrupts the original ideas and perspectives, and occasionally deleting passages now apparently considered inadequate or outdated.[1] The transformations in Freud's psychoanalytic thought thus found their way into the various editions. As a result of this, the final 1924 edition is not simply the 'best' version in a series of editions in which, as Freud himself states in the preface to the second edition when he writes: 'what was imperfect may be replaced by something better'. It is much more a layered composition of theories and theoretical elements that presents itself as an archaeological site – to use one of Freud's well-known metaphors for psychoanalytic work – that needs to be excavated in order to expose the deepest, oldest layer. This volume can be read as an exhibition of several of the most important findings unearthed from that oldest layer – the 1905 edition of the *Three Essays*.

As self-evident as such excavation work might seem, a study of the literature on Freudian psychoanalysis in general and his theory on sexuality in particular shows that most scholars take the final version of the *Three Essays* to be the officially approved and most authoritative one.[2] Yet reading the *Three Essays* in its final version as if it is merely the 'better' or 'best' version proves to have tremendous and problematic implications for the evaluation of Freudian theory, its development, and the place and status of the *Three Essays* in this context. A quick look at the later inserted material – the various younger layers – soon reveals the problems one is confronted with when dealing with this text. One finds that Freud added large paragraphs on the drive and libido theory, on the child's sexual researches, on the castration complex, on the phases of development of the sexual organization, the child's ambivalent feelings and the diphasic object choice, on the influence of phylogenetic material, and – in some scattered footnotes – on narcissism and the Oedipus complex. Freud presents these issues as essential parts of the theory of infantile and adult sexuality in the later editions of the text. Yet they are not only virtually absent in the 1905 first version, they are actually issues that fundamentally redefine infantile sexuality and its relation to adult sexuality.

There is no need to explore these issues and their implications in detail in the context of this introduction, for they will be further discussed throughout the various contributions to this volume, and we will draw some general conclusions regarding these issues in the epilogue. What needs to be addressed in this introduction is the fact that because the final version of the *Three Essays* has, down to the present day, been largely taken as the authoritative one, the normalizing, heteronormative elements in the text have been put to the fore. This has two important implications. First, Freud's original perspective on infantile sexuality has been largely covered over by subsequent layers of the later theory in which the infant's object choice and the submission to cultural norms became more central. Second, the *Three Essays* could then be used to support a more general – and problematic – evaluation of Freudian theory in which his early work is seen to be in accordance with the later, supposedly more mature theory. Were the references to breast-sucking not a clear indication that Freud had been under the spell of oedipal thinking ever since he abandoned the seduction theory in 1897? Did not each 'better' version of the *Three Essays* only make more explicit the psychoanalytic shibboleth(s) that had always been at the centre of Freud's thought? The fundamental problem with such views quickly becomes evident when reading the 1905 edition: if infantile sexuality is without a (real or phantasmatic) object – as Freud claims in 1905 – how could it ever then be characterized as 'oedipal'?

It is not only psychoanalytic scholarship but also the philosophical critique of the psychoanalytic theory of sexuality that is shaped by the fact that the first version of the *Three Essays* was largely concealed by later theoretical and methodological developments. The writings of Michel Foucault, for example, confront us with this ambiguity. In his early work on the history of madness, *Histoire de la folie à l'âge classique* (1961), he notices that Freud broke away from traditional psychiatry in at least one respect, namely by restoring the dialogue with and experience of unreason and madness to medical thought, which had for so long sought to silence, disguise or confine madness (Foucault 2009). In his later writings on the history of sexuality, he further develops this insight into the rupture made manifest in psychoanalysis in claiming that Freudian psychoanalysis opposed itself to nineteenth-century psychiatry and sexology, and thus made possible a new way of thinking about sexuality. Nevertheless, although he reached exactly the point where he could have taken his view of psychoanalysis one step further by delving into the content of Freud's early theory of sexuality as a theory of the body and its pleasures, Foucault instead chose to highlight the continuity of psychoanalysis with a Christian and later secular tradition in which the body with its impulses, excitations and pleasures is submitted to regimes of power and control through language and knowledge in various practices, regulations and institutions (Foucault 2003). Psychoanalysis appears in this long history as a new technique of normalization which, according to Foucault, not by coincidence introduces the Oedipus complex at the historical moment, the end of the nineteenth century, when family life is discovered by the juridical system as a locus of unwanted intimacies (Foucault 1979). It is indeed oedipal thought that is at the heart of the Foucauldian critique of psychoanalysis – a critique that links him to Deleuze and Guattari's (1977) *Anti-Oedipus*. The problem these thinkers address is not so much the clinical material confirming oedipal desires and relations as such, but the use of the oedipus complex as an instrument of normalization of pleasure and desire in and through the family structure (Basaure 2009). According to Foucault, it is at exactly this point that Freud fails to initiate a break with the traditional *scientia sexualis* and actually continues its most fundamental ideas. After all, a medico-biological theory of the natural organization of the sexual instincts and its degenerate aberrations, and a psychoanalytic theory highlighting a cultural structure (the nuclear family) as the normal organizational form of sexuality result in the same heteronormativity and identification of certain sexual tendencies as abnormal aberrations. The question that thus arises is whether Freud's theory of sexuality is an oedipal theory. It is exactly in view of this question that the first version of the *Three Essays* is of crucial importance.

Foucault's interpretations of Freudian psychoanalysis provide us with a good view of what is at stake when reading the *Three Essays*. What exactly is the relation between the 1905 *Three Essays* and the psychiatric and sexological literature of Freud's predecessors? How does Freud redefine sexuality and the perversions, the relation between pathology and normality, the body and its drives, pleasures and needs, and the relation between constitution and culture? Should the original and radical nature of Freud's text only be understood in relation to the writings of his predecessors, or can it also be seen – perhaps more interestingly – in relation to a whole body of later oedipal psychoanalytic thought? Can we, so to speak, read Freud against Freud and Freudians? And if so, what would be the relevance and actuality of the 1905 edition of the *Three Essays* for contemporary thought on sexuality, pleasure, perversion, pathology and normality? These and other related questions are at the heart of the seven chapters in this volume.

In the first two chapters of this volume *Rachel Blass* and *Herman Westerink* explore and discuss the central concepts, the main composition of ideas relative to the contemporary psychiatric and sexological literature, and the most important theoretical and methodological aspects of the 1905 edition of the *Three Essays*. Blass elaborates a fundamental tension in Freud's thinking concerning human sexuality as both inherently object-related and inherently independent of this relatedness. Westerink focuses on the originality and radicality of Freud's theory of sexuality and describes what theoretical problems forced him to reformulate his ideas in the later editions of the text. In the third chapter, *Harry Oosterhuis* situates the *Three Essays* in the larger context of the modernization of sexuality by focusing on two pioneers of sexual theory, Richard von Krafft-Ebing and Albert Moll. In their writings, it is possible to identify new conceptualizations and classifications of sexuality that foreshadow Freud's views on sexuality. Thus Oosterhuis emphasizes the continuity between Freud and his predecessors. In his contribution, *Patrick Vandermeersch* examines a crucial sentence in the 1905 edition of *Three Essays* that is deleted from the later versions: the first 'definition' of the sexual drive. He argues that we must understand the erasure of this sentence in the context of Freud's debate with Jung on psychosis, drive and sexuality. *Jens De Vleminck* develops a brief genealogy of sadism and masochism in his contribution to this volume. He argues that Freud's reconceptualization of these phenomena is problematic in the context of the prevalence of the paradigm of hysteria in the *Three Essays*. In the next chapter, *Monique David-Ménard* focuses on the ambiguity of Freud's basic clinical and conceptual vocabulary that ultimately resulted in the normalization of sexuality by psychoanalysis. This ambiguity concerns the notion of the drive as defined relative to both autoerotism and object-relatedness. *Philippe Van Haute* highlights the role of the perversions in Freud's *Three Essays* and confronts Freud's patho-analytic approach with Lacan's reference to a perverse structure that seems to (re-)introduce the idea of the pervert subject having a different identity. The latter position supports the heteronormativity that Freud criticized in his 1905 theory of infantile sexuality. A short epilogue concludes this volume.

This volume is the result of a conference entitled 'Deconstructing Normativity. Re-reading Freud's *Three Essays*' held in November 2014 at the Center for Contemporary European Philosophy, Radboud University, Nijmegen, the Netherlands. The conference and volume are part of a larger project that includes new translations and text editions (in German, English and Dutch) of the 1905 version of the *Three Essays*, and a monograph on the various editions of the *Three Essays* in which we investigate from a philosophical perspective the transformations in Freud's theory of sexuality relative to the development of his psychoanalytic thought and in the broader context of developments in psychiatry, sexology and other relevant scientific fields.

We would like to thank Andrew Smith, Beatriz Santos and Arjen Kleinherenbrink for their excellent and meticulous correction and editorial work.

Notes

1 There is also a 1925 edition published at Deuticke Verlag, but there are no changes between this and the 1924 edition published in the *Gesammelte Schriften*.
2 This is mirrored by the fact that in the *Gesammelte Werke* we find the edition of 1924 with neither references to the deleted passages nor any indication for those that were inserted later. In the *Standard Edition* and the *Studienausgabe* we do find these references and markings, yet, in such a way that it proves difficult to have a clear view of the original text while reading it. At this point, we should note that there is no historical critical edition of Freud's work, and – more importantly in this respect – no English translation of the first edition. Abraham Brill translated the 1910 edition into English and James Strachey the 1924 edition. A more recent translation by Shaun Whiteside is also based on the 1924 edition and was published in 2006 as part of the Freud series edited by Adam Phillips under the title, *Three Essays on Sexual Theory* (in the volume *The Psychology of Love*. London: Penguin).

References

Basaure, M. (2009). Foucault and the 'Anti-Oedipus Movement': Psychoanalysis as Disciplinary Power. *History of Psychiatry* 20:3, 340–359.
Deleuze, G. and Guattari, F. (1977). *Anti-Oedipus: Capitalism et Schizophrenia*. New York: Penguin Viking.
Foucault, M. (2009). *History of Madness*. New York: Routledge.
Foucault, M. (1979). *The History of Sexuality I: The Will to Knowledge*. London: Allen Lane.
Foucault, M. (2003). *Abnormal: Lectures at the Collège de France 1974–1975*. New York: Picador.
Freud, S. (1905). *Three Essays on the Theory of Sexuality*, J. Strachey (ed.), *Standard Edition 7*. London: Hogarth.

1

UNDERSTANDING FREUD'S CONFLICTED VIEW OF THE OBJECT-RELATEDNESS OF SEXUALITY[1] AND ITS IMPLICATIONS FOR CONTEMPORARY PSYCHOANALYSIS

A re-examination of Three Essays on the Theory of Sexuality

Rachel Blass

Introduction

The nature of the role of the object in Freud's thinking is one that has always been subject to question and debate. Emphasizing his ideas on primary narcissism and autoerotism, many have stressed that Freud regarded the relationship to the object as something that evolves developmentally. Freud's "amoeba metaphor", first introduced in his "On Narcissism", is often adduced in this context. He writes:

> Thus we form the idea of there being an original libidinal cathexis of the ego, from which some is later given off to objects, but which fundamentally persists and is related to the object-cathexes much as the body of an amoeba is related to the pseudopodia which it puts out. In our researches, taking, as they did, neurotic symptoms for their starting-point, this part of the allocation of libido necessarily remained hidden from us at the outset. All that we noticed were the emanations of this libido – the object-cathexes, which can be sent out and drawn back again.
>
> *(Freud 1914: 75)*

According to this view of Freud, he maintained that counter to how things may have seemed at first, the individual is not inherently object-related. He is determined by his instincts, but the object is not integral to the instincts and it is not towards the object that the instincts are necessarily directed. Rather the individual enters into a relationship with objects through their gradual cathexis with libido and their subsequent internalization. Those who hold this view include both critics and supporters of the position ascribed to Freud (e.g. relational psychoanalysts and ego psychologists alike). Freud's comments on the object in his 1915 "Instincts and Their Vicissitudes" provide similar support of this view:

> Originally, at the very beginning of mental life, the ego is cathected with instincts ... At this time the external world is not cathected with interest ... but, in consequence of experiences undergone by the instincts of self-preservation, it acquires objects from that world.
>
> *(Freud 1915: 135–136)*

In contrast, there are those who maintain that Freud considers object-relatedness to be inherent and primary. Two senses of primacy come into play here. Some refer to a temporal primacy, arguing that the individual according to Freud is object-related from the start and that his positions on narcissism and autoeroticism must be interpreted in light of this primacy as certain forms of relatedness; for example, autoeroticism should be regarded as a reproduction of an earlier object relationship with the mother (Heimann 1952: 145).[2] Others refer to primacy in the sense of significance. They allow for the idea that Freud indeed posited unrelated states, but maintain that his ideas in this regard were secondary to the contradictory position that he held on the individual being inherently and originally object-related. Melanie Klein among others seems to hold to this view, openly acknowledging that there is tension in Freud's thinking on this matter (Klein 1952: 52). She writes: "As regards autoerotism and narcissism we meet with an inconsistency in Freud's views ... Freud had not yet arrived at a final decision". She goes on to state that her differences are therefore not so much with Freud, but with Anna Freud who took up only the non-object-related side of Freud's thinking.

Those who hold to the object-related view of Freud's thinking readily adduce in its support the centrality that Freud ascribes to the Oedipus complex, its interpersonal dynamics and prehistorical origins. The Oedipus complex is grounded in the idea that the individual comes into the world already identified with objects from what Freud refers to as "his own personal prehistory" (Freud 1923: 30). This is a relationship which Freud explains:

> [t]akes place earlier than any object-cathexis. But the object-choices belonging to the first sexual period and relating to the father and mother seem normally to find their outcome in an identification of this kind, and would thus reinforce the primary one.
>
> *(Freud 1923: 31)*

In line with this view, Freud writes in his "Group Psychology and the Analysis of the Ego":

> It is true that individual psychology is concerned with the individual man and explores the paths by which he seeks to find satisfaction for his instinctual impulses; but only rarely and under certain exceptional conditions is individual psychology in a position to disregard the relations of this individual to others. In the individual's mental life someone else is invariably involved, as a model, as an object, as a helper, as an opponent; and so from the very first individual psychology ... is at the same time social psychology as well.
>
> (Freud 1921: 69)

In other words, the individual as a psychological being is to be regarded in terms of his instinctual impulses, but these are inherently tied to an object. The individual is relational. Freud does not forget narcissistic states here, but rather he regards these as exceptional states of *withdrawal* of the instinct from the influence of other people, not as primary and original (Freud 1921: 69).

This chapter is an examination of Freud's thinking on the role of object in his *Three Essays on the Theory of Sexuality*. As I will show, Freud's reflections on the nature of sexuality in this book contain some of his most direct and forceful statements on the role of the object, but interestingly these statements go both ways. They emphasize both (a) the individual's primary unrelatedness, his sexual instincts being basically independent of object relations, and (b) the fact that the individual and his sexuality are fundamentally object-related from the start. Moreover, Freud presents these seemingly opposing positions in a complex, self-contradictory way and without making any effort to reconcile them. I will suggest that this sheds light on Freud's approach to the role of the object, pointing to the fact that it was an inherently conflicted one. Both prevalent interpretations of Freud's writing are misguided. That is, in order to understand Freud one need not only to understand each of his positions on the role of the object and determine their relative importance, but also to understand the meaning of the conflict between them. We are faced with the questions: By placing in juxtaposition such contradictory views, what was Freud trying to tell us about human nature? What can be learned from this about psychoanalytic thinking then and also now and especially what can be learned about object-relatedness and sexuality?

Returning to *Three Essays*

The *Three Essays* is a very important text for Freud, one of the few (like *The Interpretation of Dreams* (Freud 1900)) which he was careful to revise and re-revise over a period of many years. More broadly, it is an important *psychoanalytic* text, central to the understanding of psychoanalytic ideas on sexuality, its infantile origins, its development throughout the stages of life and its perversions. James Strachey, in his introduction to its English translation, refers to the *Three Essays* as Freud's "most momentous and original contributions to human knowledge", second only to his *Interpretation of Dreams* (Freud 1900: 126). While Strachey goes on to wonder about the impact of the text at the time of its first publication, it would seem to me that another significant question is its contemporary relevance. With so many of its main theses and claims regarding sexuality (e.g. its early onset, the fact that it has diverse, non-genital expressions in all of us, and the natural presence of homosexuality, bisexuality and perversion) having been integrated into mainstream analytic thinking, what may have been ground-breaking in Freud's time may seem obvious, almost banal, in our own.

I turned to examine this question following an invitation to present a lecture at a conference on the *Three Essays*. And in fact it was the lecture commitment that kept me focused on this task despite what I experienced to be Freud's unpleasant, perhaps even boring, writing style in this text. More so than any other of Freud's works (and by far), the *Three Essays* comes across as very dense and dry, medical and impersonal. Perseverance with the task, however, made me increasingly aware of the text's underlying richness and relevance, which to a large extent was tied to Freud's complex ideas on the role of object-relatedness in sexuality that are put forth in its course. When one begins to wonder about what Freud is saying about these roles, the text becomes quite interesting and deep.

Before now presenting my findings on Freud's ideas on the object in the *Three Essays*, I would like to highlight some of the difficulties with the text's style. This may not only help others to better contend with the text but also is, as we shall see, relevant to the understanding of the content of Freud's ideas. I will conclude by indicating one way in which Freud's thinking impacts contemporary questions facing psychoanalysis' understanding of sexuality. This has to do with the question of the evaluation of sexual practices as normal or abnormal.

The dry presentation of sexuality in the *Three Essays*

The dominant tone of the *Three Essays* is a medical (as opposed to a personal) one. Freud writes as though he were actively involved compiling extensive quantitative empirical data. For example, in referring to sexual aims, he writes:

> Among men, intercourse *per anum* by no means coincides with inversion; masturbation is quite as frequently their exclusive aim, and ... restrictions of sexual aim ... are commoner among them than among heterosexual lovers. Among women, too, the sexual aims of inverts are various: there seems to be a special preference for contact with the mucous membrane of the mouth.
> (Freud 1905: 145–146)

The same tone is maintained when Freud speaks of completely socially acceptable practices. For example, Freud refers to kissing as the bringing together of the mucous membranes of the lips (1905: 151).

Elsewhere he writes as though his concern is physiological. Speaking of the erotogenic zones he states that they are:

[u]sed to provide a certain amount of pleasure by being stimulated in the way appropriate to them. This pleasure then leads to an increase in tension which in its turn is responsible for producing the necessary motor energy for the conclusion of the sexual act. The penultimate stage of that act is once again the appropriate stimulation of an erotogenic zone (the genital zone itself, in the glans penis) by the appropriate object (the mucous membrane of the vagina); and from the pleasure yielded by this excitation the motor energy is obtained, this time by a reflex path, which brings about the discharge of the sexual substances. This last pleasure is the highest in intensity, and its mechanism differs from that of the earlier pleasure. It is brought about entirely by discharge: it is wholly a pleasure of satisfaction and with it the tension of the libido is for the time being extinguished.

This distinction between the one kind of pleasure due to the excitation of erotogenic zones and the other kind due to the discharge of the sexual substances deserves, I think, to be made more concrete by a difference in nomenclature. The former may be suitably described as "fore-pleasure" in contrast to the "end-pleasure" or pleasure of satisfaction derived from the sexual act. Fore-pleasure is thus the same pleasure that has already been produced, although on a smaller scale, by the infantile sexual instinct; end-pleasure is something new and is thus probably conditioned by circumstances that do not arise till puberty. The formula for the new function of the erotogenic zones runs therefore: they are used to make possible, through the medium of the fore-pleasure which can be derived from them (as it was during infantile life), the production of the greater pleasure of satisfaction.

(1905: 210)

Freud continues with extensive descriptions of this kind. Even when talking of what seem to be clearly very human and less physiological matters (such as emotional experience (1905: 203) and intellectual work (1905: 204)) the detached tone persists. Moreover, Freud brings no cases and no detailed descriptions of specific human relationships. There are, of course, comments on parental love and the need for the presence of loved objects (which I will soon address), but they are embedded within the prevalent technical presentation and almost exclusively presented as appearing late in the developmental process.

I now turn to the object-related questions that concerned Freud in the *Three Essays* and which find their way through his detached style, bringing his text alive. I will first present how Freud emphasizes that sexuality is not inherently object-related. The individual is motivated by instincts, but the object is not integral to them from the start. I will then show how Freud puts forth a view that stands directly opposed to this view through a series of complex and self-contradictory statements on the role of the object.

On object-relatedness in sexuality

How and why sexuality is not object-related

Freud's critique of the misguided inference regarding the inherent tie of instincts to objects

At the end of the first section of the first essay on "The Sexual Aberrations", entitled "Deviations in respect to the sexual object", in the subsection on "Inversion" Freud draws the following main conclusion:

> [w]e have been in the habit of regarding the connection between the sexual instinct and the sexual object as more intimate than it in fact is. Experience of the cases that are considered abnormal has shown us that in them the sexual instinct and the sexual object are merely soldered together – a fact which we have been in danger of overlooking in consequence of the uniformity of the normal picture, where the object appears to form part and parcel of the instinct. We are thus warned to loosen the bond that exists in our thoughts between instinct and object. It seems probable that the sexual instinct is in the first instance independent of its object; nor is its origin likely to be due to its object's attractions.
>
> *(1905: 147–148)*

This reference to the sexual instinct being independent of the object seems to quite directly support the notion that the object is not inherent to sexual instincts and that Freud considered object relations secondary, later developments. Freud tells us of our misguided tendency to consider sexual drives as inherently tied to objects, but it is one that we should overcome. We should, he affirms, "loosen the bond that exists in our thoughts between instinct and object" (1905: 148). In effect, Freud says here that the sexual instinct, in essence, is a kind of objectless force that merely latches onto objects as one of the kinds of things that it does. In normal cases they are *soldered* together in a way that may lead us to perceive an inherent tie, but this is not really the case.

In the following subsection headed "Sexually immature persons and animals as sexual objects", Freud describes a lack of apparent connection between having an abnormal sexual life and having mental abnormalities (although those with mental abnormalities will invariably have abnormal sexual lives). To explain this, he puts forth the view "that the impulses of sexual life are among those which, even normally are the least controlled by the higher activities of mind" (1905: 149). While one might have suggested that Freud here is laying emphasis on detachment of the sexual and the mental only in regard to the "higher" activities of the mental, his following paragraph puts such an interpretation in doubt. He writes:

> The most general conclusion that follows from all these discussions seems, however, to be this. Under a great number of conditions and in surprisingly numerous individuals, the nature and importance of the sexual object recedes

into the background. What is essential and constant in the sexual instinct is something else.

(1905: 149)

He concludes the section with these enigmatic words regarding the essence of the instinct and in a footnote added five years later again refers to something in the instinct itself that is not tied to the object, without specifying what this something is. He writes:

> The most striking distinction between the erotic life of antiquity and our own no doubt lies in the fact that the ancients laid the stress upon the instinct itself, whereas we emphasize its object. The ancients glorified the instinct and were prepared on its account to honour even an inferior object; while we despise the instinctual activity in itself, and find excuses for it only in the merits of the object.
>
> *(1905: 149)*

From autoerotism to object choice – the limited role of the object

This line of thinking is continued in the next essay on "Infantile Sexuality" as Freud begins to address the issue of autoerotism. Regarding the study of thumb sucking as a way to understand the essence of infantile sexuality, Freud writes:

> It must be insisted that the most striking feature of this sexual activity [the infantile kind] is that the instinct is not directed towards other people, but obtains satisfaction from the subject's own body. It is "auto-erotic", to call it by a happily chosen term introduced by Havelock Ellis (1910).
>
> *(1905: 181)*

Taking note of the apparent presence of an object in the stories of seduction that Freud's patients had supposedly reported, Freud explains that:

> [t]he effects of seduction do not help to reveal the early history of the sexual instinct; they rather confuse our view of it by presenting children prematurely with a sexual object for which the infantile sexual instinct at first shows no need.
>
> *(1905: 191)*

Freud qualifies this statement, but only slightly:

> It must, however, be admitted that infantile sexual life, in spite of the preponderating dominance of erotogenic zones, exhibits components which from the very first involve other people as sexual objects. Such are the

instincts of scopophilia, exhibitionism and cruelty, which appear in a sense independently of erotogenic zones.

(1905: 191–192)

Freud goes on to argue that (barring these exceptions) the choice of an object takes place in two phases; the first takes place between the ages of two and five and the second in puberty. And in line with his ongoing approach of downplaying the role of the object, when he comes to his third essay on "The Transformations of Puberty", he almost forgets the first of these phases. Thus he opens the essay: "With the arrival of puberty, changes set in which are destined to give infantile sexual life its final, normal shape. The sexual instinct has hitherto been predominantly auto-erotic; it now finds a sexual object" (1905: 207). In this statement it would seem as though it is only in *puberty* that an object is found.

Freud's contradictory position on the object-relatedness of sexuality

The limited and late role that Freud attributes to the object stands in sharp contrast to another view that Freud strongly puts forth on this matter and in the very same text, namely, the view that the object is inherent to the individual and his sexuality. But, as we shall see, Freud's affirmation of this object-related view is presented in a contradictory way; one which repeatedly brings to mind his non-object-related position as well.

Object-relatedness in autoerotism

One clear example of this may be seen in Freud's understanding of autoerotism. While (as we have seen) Freud emphasizes that "the most striking feature" of the infantile sexual instinct is that it is not directed towards other people but towards one's own body, a few lines later Freud adds that the turn to the body is "determined by a search for some pleasure which has already been experienced and is now remembered". And what is that earlier pleasure? Freud writes:

> It is also easy to guess the occasions on which the child had his first experiences of the pleasure which he is now striving to renew. It was the child's first and most vital activity, his sucking at his mother's breast, or at substitutes for it, that must have familiarized him with this pleasure.
>
> *(1905: 181)*

Here Freud seems to be speaking quite directly of autoerotism being founded on an earlier object relationship. Indeed, as noted earlier, that is how Kleinians, who wish to ground their thinking in Freud's, read him. Paula Heimann in her 1943 (published in 1952) controversial discussion paper "Certain Functions of Introjection and Projection in Early Infancy" writes that:

> When analysing the infants' autoerotic sucking Freud pointed out that it rests upon an experience with an object, the mother's breast, which has acquainted the infant with a pleasure which he later reproduces autoerotically. At first, according to Freud, infantile libido is attached to an object and amalgamated with feeding; later it becomes detached both from this self-preservative function and from the object. Freud did not here enter in the question of what happens in the infant's mind when he abandons the object.
>
> (Heimann 1952: 145)

She goes on to comment how, of course, in "Mourning and Melancholia" (Freud 1917a), Freud does address this question and explained how "the abandoned object is established within the ego, introjected" (Heimann 1952: 145).

Interestingly, however, it is already in the *Three Essays* that Freud speaks of introjection. This is in a section added in 1915. Regarding the oral phase, Freud states:

> Here sexual activity has not yet been separated from the ingestion of food ... the sexual aim consists in the incorporation of the object – the prototype of a process which, in the form of identification, is later to play such an important psychological part.
>
> (Freud 1905: 198)

In this context, speaking of thumb sucking, he again reiterates the primacy of the object: "The sexual activity, detached from the nutritive activity, has substituted for the extraneous object one situated in the subject's own body" (1905: 198).[3]

The contrast with Freud's comments on the instinct as object-free and autoerotic from the start is quite striking. But this conflict becomes ever-more striking because the object-relatedness that Freud here describes seems to shift between a personal and loving form of relatedness to the object and a detached use of the object as a source of stimulation of the erotogenic zones. For example, immediately after stating that autoerotic pleasure is an attempt to renew the most vital activity of sucking at the mother's breast, Freud adds (in his dryer and more detached tone) that: "the child's lips, in our view, behave like an erotogenic zone, and no doubt stimulation by the warm flow of milk is the cause of the pleasurable sensation" (1905: 181). That is, it is the warm sensation on the lips rather than the mother object that seems to be the relevant factor in Freud's mind.

In this context, of special interest also is Freud's very famous statement that "The finding of an object is in fact a re-finding of it" (1905: 222), a statement made in the third of the *Three Essays* as Freud discusses "The finding of an object" in puberty. This statement seems to provide the clearest evidence of Freud's awareness of the primacy of the object. However, one may see that even in this dramatic statement there is a certain ambiguity that reveals a more ambivalent stance. In the lines directly preceding this famous quote, Freud refers (as he does earlier in the text) to the mother's breast as the child's first object and autoerotism as a consequence of loss of that first object. And he adds now that "a child sucking at his mother's breast has become the prototype of every relation of love" (1905: 222) – yet another apparently object-related statement. But, at the same time, Freud states that the original loss of the breast takes place "just at the time, perhaps, when the child is able to form a total idea of the person to whom the organ that is giving him satisfaction belongs" (1905: 222) – that is, the primary relationship is to a stimulating and satisfying organ, not to the *mother's* breast. Moreover, Freud strangely refers to the loss that takes place as a loss by the instinct. It is "the instinct", not the baby, that "loses the object".

Oedipal object relations

Freud's conflicted position regarding the tie between instinct and object, the central and primary role that he ascribes to the object alongside his minimization of its role, may be seen not only in the opposing positions he puts forth regarding the early autoerotic phase. It may also be seen in how he regards the oedipal dynamics in this text. As noted earlier, Freud's oedipal model relies on the notion of primary identifications with objects, prior to object cathexis. But in the *Three Essays*, Freud's approach to this model is rather complicated.

It is in this text that Freud makes his strongest and most famous statement on the centrality of oedipal dynamics. He writes:

> It has justly been said that the Oedipus complex is the nuclear complex of the neuroses, and constitutes the essential part of their content. It represents the peak of infantile sexuality, which, through its after-effects, exercises a decisive influence on the sexuality of adults. Every new arrival on this planet is faced by the task of mastering the Oedipus complex; anyone who fails to do so falls a victim to neuroses. With the progress of psycho-analytic studies the importance of the Oedipus complex has become more and more clearly evident; its recognition has become the shibboleth that distinguishes the adherents of psycho-analysis from its opponents.
>
> *(1905: 226)*

In other words, Freud directly states that one can identify a true follower of psychoanalysis by his recognition of the importance of the Oedipus complex. This seems to be unequivocal support of the ultimate centrality of this object-relational complex, and yet on closer reading one can find even here Freud's contradictory stance. First, this comment is added only in 1920 and even then only as a footnote. Second, this belated footnote is notably out of sync with the general gist of the *Three Essays*, which actually almost completely disregards the complex. The facts are that (a) there are only three brief direct references to it, (b) all are in footnotes and (c) the other references to parents and parental love that one finds in the *Three Essays* (i.e. aside from the footnotes) suggest that Freud was not thinking of parent-child relationships in what is commonly thought to be oedipal terms.

What one finds from a close reading of these references, rather, is that parental love and love of parents are regarded as states that emerge in the effort to satisfy the instincts, not as something inherent to the instincts.

These references appear mainly towards the very end of the text, in the third essay in the section entitled "The finding of an object". There, for example, Freud writes of the child's love of the mother in what may seem at first to be a typical oedipal description of the relationship between the two. He states:

> All through the period of latency children learn to feel for other people who help them in their helplessness and satisfy their needs a love which is on the model of, and a continuation of, their relation as sucklings to their nursing mother . . . A child's intercourse with anyone responsible for his care affords him an unending source of sexual excitation and satisfaction from his erotogenic zones.
>
> *(1905: 222–223)*

While this description may seem to be oedipal, the fact is that Freud here speaks of sexual love towards parents as something that is *learned*, not given (albeit based on an early relationship), and moreover, as something which would be felt towards *anyone* who happened to sexually excite the young child.

A bit later in speaking of "the barrier against incest", another seemingly typical oedipal theme, Freud explains that the child's choice of his parents as objects would be "the *simplest* course" (1905: 225, my italics), not the psychically determined *natural* one. And Freud goes on to claim that the incestuous object choice is put aside out of respect for a cultural demand to do so and that this move is made possible by the delay of physical sexual maturation that gives the child time "to erect . . . the barrier against incest" (1905: 225). Only in 1915 does Freud add a brief footnote to this section that may remind the reader that elsewhere Freud held a more apparently oedipal view of the incest barrier, based not on contemporary and external cultural demands, but ancient and internal ones, and even this footnote is somewhat tentative (stating that "the barrier against incest is *probably* among the historical acquisitions of mankind" and that it has "become established in *many* persons by organic inheritance" (1905: 225, my italics)).[4]

It should be added that oedipal dynamics are also notably absent in Freud's discussion of pathology in the *Three Essays*.

Making sense of the contradictions

In sum, I contend that what has been described here strongly suggests that the *Three Essays* attests to a serious problem in Freud's thinking in regard to the individual's basic object-relatedness. The text is riddled with tension, apparent both through contradictory positions taken within the text and wide gaps between Freud's positions within the text and those he held elsewhere. Indeed, in the *Three Essays* Freud makes statements that suggest he was committed to an object-related perspective, but Freud's statements to the contrary make it quite clear that Freud did not simply embrace an object-related perspective (like Klein's), neither was he merely "not unequivocal" on the matter (Klein 1952: 51). The fact is that he openly espouses the idea of a primary autoerotism and narcissism and at the very same time acknowledges an inherent tie between instinct and object. This calls for explanation. How are we to make sense of the contradictions and gaps? What is the meaning of the intense struggle that seems to be going on below the dry and impersonal surface of the *Three Essays?*

It is striking that for the most part the contradictions go unnoticed in the analytic literature. As I have argued elsewhere (Blass 1992: 183–184), there is a tendency to read Freud's famous texts in terms of what he is conventionally thought to have said or what he should have said to be consistent with the Freudian frameworks to which we have grown accustomed. Often, where Freud strays from those frameworks, he is ignored or little meaning is ascribed to his deviations. This seems, in part, to account for the neglect of the tensions in the *Three Essays*. For example, Jean-Michel Quinodoz in his very important introductory book, *Reading Freud* (Quinodoz 2005), refers to the lack of mention of the Oedipus complex in the 1905 edition of the *Three Essays*, but notes that this was corrected in the later editions. Interestingly, he concludes his chapter on the *Three Essays* with a two-page summary of the development of the Oedipus complex based on other texts, perhaps in this way conveying that Freud *must* have been speaking of the Oedipus complex since it is so intimately tied to infantile sexuality (2005: 58). This, I think, is a widespread sentiment in the analytic community. As Moses Laufer explains in a paper presented in 1980: "The link between the *Three Essays* and the concept of the Oedipus complex is an obvious one because, for Freud, the relationship between sexuality and the Oedipus complex was inseparable" (Laufer 1982: 217). It is significant that he makes these remarks at a plenary session on the Oedipus complex that the International Psychoanalytical Association organized to "honour and acknowledge" the *Three Essays* on the occasion of the 75th anniversary of its publication. Freud's ideas on the inherent tie of sexuality to oedipal object relations are acknowledged. His simultaneous denial of the tie is neglected.

The evolutionary solution to some of the contradictions and its limitations

Despite the general neglect of the contradictions in the *Three Essays*, some authors have taken note of them and tried to explain them. Most notable in this regard are Laplanche and Pontalis. While it would seem that they do not fully address the problems with Freud's thinking on autoerotism (Laplanche & Pontalis 1973: 45–47)[5] they do comment on the blatant disregard of the Oedipus complex (see also Compton 1981: 225). They understand this disregard in terms of Freud's evolving theory following his disillusionment with his seduction theory. I think that this is a legitimate direction of explanation. In fact, I too, in a different way, have argued that counter to analytic lore Freud's path from the seduction theory to the Oedipus complex was a long and difficult one. As I have shown (Blass 1992; Blass & Simon 1994), it was not the discovery of the Oedipus complex that entailed the abandonment of the seduction theory (or theories – Freud never had *one* such theory). Rather, having put in question the role of the seducer in engendering pathological conflict, Freud explored several alternative theories that would explain its appearance and his thinking had to significantly develop before he could arrive at an oedipal understanding of conflict. In the *Three Essays*, his main solution (which he also applies in the Dora case) is that "when infantile drives retain their initial force, later conflict will result in pathology … the antithesis between infantile strivings and mature demands sets the scene for pathogenic conflict. In the absence of sublimation, pathology ensues" (Blass 1992: 180).

It is interesting that this move away from explanation in terms of seduction was not only a step *towards* the recognition of the role of the oedipal object, but also step *away* from it. With the seducer excluded, personal (rather than external) responsibility was emphasized to the point that "the idea of 'the father' as an inherent component of the girl's inner fantasy world could not emerge" (Blass 1992: 181). That is, (as we see in the Dora case), infantile sexuality explanations of the pathological conflict involved an inward focus that downplayed the role of the object and offered alternatives to object-related explanations. Important theoretical developments were needed, prime among them Freud's phylogenetic hypothesis of *Totem and Taboo*, to tie between inner drives and inner objects.

This kind of understanding of the gradual evolution of Freud's ideas may partially explain the absence of the Oedipus complex in the first, 1905, edition of the *Three Essays*.[6] But its failure to explain its absence in the later editions is glaring. This is for two main reasons: first, Freud was constantly updating the *Three Essays*. He could have brought the text up to date. Not only did he not do this but he almost openly informs the reader that he refuses to do so. He inserts a footnote on the universality of the Oedipus complex (to recall: "every new arrival on this planet is faced by the task of mastering the Oedipus complex"), its central role in neuroses ("anyone who fails to do so falls a victim to neuroses") and the concern with it being the defining feature of psychoanalysis ("its recognition has become the shibboleth that distinguishes the adherents of psycho-analysis from its opponents" (Freud 1905: 226)). But then in practice, in his description of the neuroses in the *Three Essays* he simply leaves it out. One might have expected that he would either refrain from such far-reaching assertions regarding the Oedipus complex or alternatively demonstrate them in his work. The understanding of the gradual evolution of Freud's ideas does not explain this contradiction.

Second, and related to this, is the fact that Freud's thinking on the Oedipus complex contradicts some of the views on autoerotism that he puts forth in the *Three Essays*. As mentioned earlier, it has been pointed out that at times Freud "clearly speaks of a libidinal attachment to an object, the mother's breast, which precedes autoerotism and narcissism" (Klein 1952: 51) and that through his oedipal model he also posits the presence of objects prior to the maternal one; identifications that precede object cathexis. It is especially difficult to reconcile such internal dynamics with Freud's thinking on autoerotism as described in the *Three Essays*.

In light of this, one cannot resolve the problem of the neglect of the Oedipus complex in the *Three Essays* by simply pointing to the fact that at the time he wrote the book he had not yet elaborated his oedipal thinking. This is because once he elaborated it, many of the claims that he makes in the book become problematic (especially his thinking on autoerotism) and Freud in his central text on sexuality does not acknowledge this and does not – despite the numerous revisions and additions that he introduces – make an apparent effort to reconcile the ideas that become contradictory. We are left with a blatant inconsistency.

In sum, the minimal and contradictory role that Freud ascribes to the object in the *Three Essays* cannot be explained away by pointing to the history of the development of his ideas. We are brought, rather, to a point of reflection and must ask: Why did Freud *wish* to retain a view of sexual instincts as primarily free of objects? Why did Freud hold on to this view even when it contradicted views he openly held on the inherent relationship of the instinct to the object? It is reflection on this question that, I think, will open us to consider the contemporary relevance of Freud's *Three Essays*.

My solutions

Freud's two opposing worldviews: objects vs instincts at the grounds of human conflict

My reflections lead me in two main directions. One of these has to do with Freud's views of the basic conflict facing man. In one sense, it may be contended that the heart of this conflict was, ultimately, to be found in the Oedipus complex. As I have summarized elsewhere (Blass 2001), this is a conflict over the father, both hated for standing in the way of receiving all the mother's love and innately loved. Hence the wish to be rid of him and gain the full love of the mother can never be happily fulfilled. The wish will have to be restrained, guilt experienced for having had the wish, and a way of dealing in reality with the limitation of love found. The complex appears anew in each individual, but as a part of our "personal prehistory" in a sense it lies at the very ground of the human psyche. We come into the world with conflicted loves and a memory of guilt for having killed the beloved father, which will shape our present personal object relationships and determine their very ethical texture (Blass 2006). Acceptance of this view is "the shibboleth that distinguishes the adherents of psycho-analysis from its opponents" (Freud 1905).

But it may be suggested that in the *Three Essays*, Freud promotes a different view of man's basic conflict and that he does so through concern for a very different kind of prehistory – a prehistory of the instincts. We do not come into the world as a *tabula rasa*, or as an individual struggling with our relationships. We come into the world rather with diverse and polymorphously perverse desires, a fairly wild assortment of biologically based tendencies – perhaps one may say with an *im*personal prehistory.[7] Conflict occurs between this impersonal heritage and our personal and cultural selves. In his summary at the end of the *Three Essays*, Freud writes:

> In view of what was now seen to be the wide dissemination of tendencies to perversion we were driven to the conclusion that a disposition to perversions is an original and universal disposition of the human sexual instinct and that normal sexual behaviour is developed out of it as a result of organic changes and psychical inhibitions occurring in the course of maturation . . . Among the forces restricting the direction taken by the sexual instinct we laid emphasis upon shame, disgust, pity and the structures of morality and authority erected by society.
>
> *(Freud 1905: 231)*

This view finds some expression in Freud's later thinking on the tension between the ego instincts and the sexual instincts, when he emphasizes that the reach of the sexual instincts "extends far beyond the individual" and thus "seem to the ego to constitute a danger which threatens its self-preservation or its self-esteem" (Freud 1917b: 138).

It may be suggested here that Freud's two views of man's basic conflict do not sit well together – and yet Freud wanted to hold on to both. In this last view of the conflict, the instinctual one, the concern with the object is not central, but defensive. An interesting example of this may be seen in one of Freud's letter to Jung in 1907. In this letter, relying on his claim that the "sexual instinct is originally autoerotic" and only later is directed towards objects, he suggests that the hysteric's reports of love and even seduction at an early age may come to conceal the autoerotic trend of the instinct. Freud writes that "hysteria [sic] . . . takes as an object anything that bears the remotest relation to a normal object" (Freud–Jung 1974: 39). And in turn, from the other point of view, the object-related oedipal conflict one, we may fear the instincts, but not because of their forceful otherness or their impropriety, but because of their implications for our objects – the ones which we wish to protect and be protected from. In the one view, we are motivated by gratification-seeking impersonal forces beyond us, and in the other nothing could *ever* be impersonal – even the most objective reality is perceived via the relational prism that shapes our mind before we are ever born.

Freud, I would suggest, by failing to resolve the contradiction in his position in the *Three Essays* regarding the role of the object, invites us to attend to it and in effect asks us to maintain the two contradictory worldviews. For analysts, this means not only to carry out an intellectual feat but also an emotional one; to find a way to live with the contradiction in the analytic situation, reflect on it – perhaps to better resolve it.

The danger of sexuality being reduced to object-relatedness

Further reflection on the tension and experiencing it through Freud's text brings to the fore a second way of thinking about the contradictory views on instinct and object that Freud leaves us with in his *Three Essays*. This second way (or at least special subgroup of the first way) has to do with the fact that in making the instinct understandable in a human and interpersonal way, something of its essential nature seems to get lost. It was as though thinking of the meanings of sexuality, sexuality is *reduced* to relations. What remains of sexuality per se when its relational meaning is interpreted? In light of this, it may be suggested that Freud did not attempt to reconcile his opposing theories and views in order to avoid such reduction. One may recall here Freud's comment in the *Three Essays* that "What is essential and constant in the sexual instinct is something else", not the object (Freud 1905: 149). It would seem that more than explain what that "something else" was, Freud was concerned to flag its existence as something that is not reducible to object-related interpretations.

In this context, it may be suggested that the detached tone of the *Three Essays* is aimed precisely at that; that it was part of an effort to keep sexuality at a distance, retain its unfamiliarity, its non-object-relatedness (e.g. in talking of kissing as the bringing together of mucous membranes).

The persistence of Freud's conflict

It would seem that even after 15 years of reflection on the *Three Essays*, the tension in Freud's thinking persisted between object-related understandings of sexuality and an understanding of the person as standing alone in a battle between his strange impersonal, biological prehistory and his personal, individual strivings to live within society. At the very end of Freud's fourth preface to the *Three Essays* written in 1920, he speaks of the profound influence of raw, physical sexuality on our lives, turning to Schopenhauer for support. He writes:

> It is some time since Arthur Schopenhauer, the philosopher, showed mankind the extent to which their activities are determined by sexual impulses – *in the ordinary sense of the word*. It should surely have been impossible for a whole world of readers to banish such a startling piece of information so completely from their minds.
>
> *(1905: 134, my italics)*

But in the very next line, the last of the preface, Freud turns to yet another philosopher to provide support for the opposing more personal and loving view of the instincts and states: "Anyone who looks down with contempt upon psycho-analysis from a superior vantage-point should remember how closely the enlarged sexuality of psycho-analysis coincides with the Eros of the divine Plato" (1905: 134).

It may be suggested that Freud's conflict, so dramatically expressed in the *Three Essays*, presents the contemporary analytic reader with important questions: How are we to live and work analytically with opposing world views? How are we to think meaningfully and psychoanalytically of sexuality without reducing it to an expression of object-relatedness? Perhaps more has to be brought out in psychoanalytic thinking and practice regarding the very physical sexual texture of relatedness.

In the contemporary context, André Green's much-cited paper "Has Sexuality Anything to Do with Psychoanalysis?" (Green 1995) seems in part to be an effort in this direction, but a limited one, especially in light of my reading of the *Three Essays*. In that paper, Green voices concern regarding the reduction of sexuality to object, which he ties, in part, to the exclusive concern with objects and specifically with the breast, which typifies Kleinian psychoanalysis and which, according to Green, severely limits the breadth and centrality of sexuality. Green maintains that the limits on sexuality are not merely because object relations presents a competing focus of interest, but rather are tied to a *basic tension* between Freud's sexual theories and contemporary objection-relations theories. The latter, he claims, do away with primary narcissism and autoeroticism which Green considers integral to Freud's sexual theories. Of course, he says, the infant depends on the mother from the start (and in that sense the object is inherently involved), but in the early months, contact with her is minimal, the baby is largely in solitude and sexuality is self-directed. Moreover, sexuality, Green argues, involves an ecstatic experience of mutual pleasure that gets lost in the object-relational descriptions.

There are, however, two main problems with Green's critique. First, he does not make completely clear what he means by the aspects of sexuality that stand beyond relationship. He mentions in this context genital aims, differences between the sexes, desire, loss of control in sexual enjoyment and the biological bedrock of all these, but does not explain why they are non-relational aspects of sexuality. Second, he considers the problem to be a post-Freudian one, having to do with the distortion of Freud's thinking by object-relational approaches. He does not recognize that the problem is, rather, inherent to Freud's thinking; that the threat to Freud's theory of sexuality actually comes from *within*, from Freud's *own* thinking on object-relatedness. To grasp sexuality, Freud found it necessary to consider it in an object-relational context. He felt that doing so posed a threat to the appreciation of certain visceral aspects of sexuality, which in some sense Freud could not clearly articulate, that lay beyond object relations. Inadequately recognizing these grounds of the problem, Green's response to it is limited and unclear. He highlights the danger to sexuality and this is valuable, but his critique of post-Freudian object-relational approaches cannot be a meaningful response to this danger. He may be right that something about the inherent nature of sexuality needs to be re-found, but from what I have described it would seem that it has always needed re-finding, from the time of Freud's earliest writings.[8]

Freud's contradictory stance that emerges from the present study of the *Three Essays* demands of contemporary psychoanalysis further reflection not only on our basic notions of sexuality but also on the implications of these notions for how we consider normal and abnormal practice from a psychoanalytic perspective. To indicate directions for future study, I will conclude by briefly describing one of these implications.

The role of the object in determining the value of sexuality

It is striking that Freud has been regarded in the analytic literature as holding either radical or conservative positions on sexuality, or maintaining both, being unable to fully espouse his truly radical ideas (D'Ercole 2014). Discussing the *Three Essays*, Peter Gay writes:

> Freud's generous vision of libido made him into a psychological democrat. Since all humans share in the erotic life, all men and women are brother and sister beneath their cultural uniforms. Sexual radicals have reproached Freud for what they have called his genital ideology, for taking adult heterosexual intercourse with a tenderly loved partner and a modicum of foreplay as the ideal to [which] all humans should aspire. But since Freud uncoupled that ideal from monogamy, his ideology was deeply subversive for his time. He was no less subversive in his uncensorious, neutral stance on perversions.
>
> *(Gay 1988: 149)*

More recent studies of Freud's *Three Essays* have also acknowledged Freud's radical neutral stance on the value of sexual practices (Moss 2014; Scarfone 2014), which can be readily grounded in Freud's explicit statements. For example, Freud writes:

> No healthy person . . . can fail to make some addition that might be called perverse to the normal sexual aim and universality of this finding is in itself enough to show how inappropriate it is to use the word perversion as a term of reproach.
>
> *(Freud 1905: 160)*

But Freud is still taken to task for the way in which he defines certain practices as perverse. As Kulish and Holtzman state (Kulish & Holtzman 2014: 284): "any preponderant sexual interest in parts of the body other than the genitals; or . . . an activity aimed at anything other than heterosexual intercourse" meets Freud's criteria of perversion. This, they maintain, loads the concepts with inappropriate societal and theological considerations.

Interestingly, many of both Freud critics and supporters propose alternative object-relational criteria for the assessment of the value of sexual practice. Kulish and Holtzman go on to explain that:

> Contemporary definitions of perversion have turned away from a sole emphasis on obligatory sexuality to stress aggression, narcissism, and object relations. Argentieri (2009), for example, suggests that perversions hide and express primitive needs of fusion and contact. Kernberg (1991) and, earlier, Stoller (1975) stress the predominance of hatred and sadomasochism inherent

> in perversion ... we endorse the emphasis on aggression, humiliation, and dehumanization of the object.
>
> *(2014: 284–285)*

However, these criteria for perverse sexuality would have been outright rejected by the Freud of the *Three Essays*. Freud explicitly maintained – to a surprising degree – that aggression, narcissism and object relations were irrelevant to the evaluation of sexual practice. In fact, in the *Three Essays*, Freud only reluctantly refers to licking excrement and having intercourse with dead bodies as pathological (Freud 1905: 161). At times Freud ties homosexuality to narcissism, but its narcissistic origin seems to make it no more or less normal (1905: 145). Aggression is considered normal too (1905: 157).

I think that here it may be seen as helpful to consider Freud's thinking in terms of the opposition between the two approaches that I have outlined. When Freud considers the person in terms of his non-object-related instinct theory, then the evaluative aspect is dismissed. In a sense, no practice or orientation is, or even could be, better or worse, normal or abnormal. Within this model, Freud speaks of disgust, shame and morality, which limit sexuality, but he presents these as biological reactions, not really explaining why our biology would react that way (1905: 152–153).[9] Moreover, these reactions carry no real imperative, evaluative force. Social structures may latch on to these biological reactions to serve social objectives, but if some sexual practice arouses disgust and even if it does so universally, this, according to Freud, is no reason to discontinue the practice. Not only does he speak of disgust as "often purely conventional" (1905: 151) but also as a feeling that restricts "normal", reproductive, sexual aims.[10]

In contrast, thinking of sexuality in terms of the object-related view of sexuality, as Freud does, both here and elsewhere, inevitably introduces an evaluative stance. This is because, as we have seen, according to this view the conflict facing the individual, the oedipal one, has a strong ethical component. Within the object-relational oedipal dynamics one struggles with sexuality because to manifest it fully in relation to the maternal object would be to harm the beloved paternal object, and we feel this to be wrong. Because of our harmful intents and the remnants within us of the prehistorical actualization of such intents, we feel guilt and seek to restrain sexual wishes and live with our limitations.

In other words, Freud here does not take the general liberal stance accepted in the analytic world that a sexual practice is OK as long as it does not harm anyone or that perversion is defined by the fact that a sexual practice causes harm. Rather the value of a sexual practice, its normality, according to Freud is determined by the success with which it resolves the specific dynamics of the Oedipus complex or is an expression of its resolution. Elaboration of the broad and difficult question of what constitutes successful resolution in this context and how this is determined would take us beyond the scope of the present chapter. But still it should be emphasized that from Freud's analytic perspective it is this question that would decide what kind of practices would be considered normal or abnormal.

For example, whether or not homosexuality is normal would be determined in part by whether the procreation is regarded as integral to conflict's successful resolution. One could, of course, put aside Freud's considerations and adopt extra-analytic ones, but the choice to do so should be clear and well-justified.[11]

It should also be emphasized that where Freud is accepting of all forms of sexuality, it is not because he recognizes their value, personal or interpersonal. Rather it is because he has completely bracketed the question of value.

One may conclude here that the two opposing readings of Freud's evaluative approach to sexual practice one finds in the literature may be a consequence or reflection of the two opposing views that Freud held on the object-relatedness of sexuality. Furthermore, one may conclude that recognizing he held two views would not only allow for a more accurate portrayal of Freud's thinking, it would also allow contemporary analysis to contend with questions having to do with the grounds of the evaluative stances it takes on sexual practice and whether such stances should, or psychoanalytically could, be taken.

Conclusion

In this paper I have shown how underlying the impersonal tone of the *Three Essays* one finds Freud struggling with two contradictory views of the person, of sexuality and of object-relatedness. The contradiction is central to the text and integral to Freud's thinking. This suggests that we may miss something basic when we view Freud only in terms of being on one or the other side of the contradiction, e.g. when we consider Freud to be essentially object-related or as essentially non-object-related. Whether this comes about from an effort to make Freud more coherent than he is or from seeking to ground our contemporary analytic approaches in Freud or to set them apart, viewing Freud in this way constricts our understanding of him and of the important issues (including evaluative ones) that he was contending with and which he invites us to contend with. That is, in his writings and notably in his *Three Essays*, Freud not only talks about conflict, he lives it and manifests it, and in so doing calls upon the reader, the contemporary reader as the reader of his own time, to directly encounter it.

Notes

1 By the term "sexuality" I refer to the person in so far as he is a sexual, instinctual, desiring, psychological being. The term has some ambiguity and may be misleading in light of certain contemporary uses of the term (e.g. in the sense of sexual orientation) but the alternatives (e.g. sexual activity, instinct, experience, etc.) were less appropriate and this is the broad and ambiguous term Freud himself opted for in the title of the *Three Essays*.
2 In this context, Klein's comments on the differences between her use of the term "object" and Freud's are interesting. While emphasizing that Freud posits primary object relations, not autoerotism, she adds that:

> Freud's use of the term object is here somewhat different from my use of this term, for he is referring to the object of an instinctual aim, while I mean, in addition to

this, an object-relation involving the infant's emotions, phantasies, anxieties, and defences. Nevertheless ... Freud clearly speaks of a libidinal attachment to an object, the mother's breast, which precedes auto-erotism and narcissism.

(Klein 1952: 435)

3 Freud's concern here with sexuality as tied to ingestion and pleasure is particularly interesting in light of the view which he soon develops of sexuality as essentially masculine (sending out rather than taking in) and altruistic (preserving the species, rather than oneself).
4 Freud's emphasis in the third preface (of 1909) that in this book his concern is with ontogenesis, not phylogenesis, is relevant in this context (Freud 1905: 131).
5 E.g. Laplanche and Pontalis simply state that Freud's theory of autoeroticism posited a primary object. They write that it:

[d]oes not assume the existence of a primitive, "objectless" state. The action of sucking, which Freud takes as the model of auto-erotism, is in fact preceded by a first stage during which the sexual instinct obtains satisfaction through an anaclitic relationship with the self-preservative instinct (hunger), and by virtue of an object – namely, the mother's breast. Only when it becomes detached from hunger does the oral sexual instinct lose its object and, by the same token, become auto-erotic.

(Laplanche and Pontalis 1973: 46)

6 It does so only partially because it is clear throughout the text that Freud not only downplays the object, but outright has as an agenda to correct our misguided conception of the value of the object (as may be seen from some of the earlier quotes).
7 Ricoeur uses the term "prehistory" in this context, but seems to tie the prehistory of the instincts to that of *Totem and Taboo*, which contains the object-related story (Ricoeur 1970).
8 In this context, one may consider Laplanche's (1970) view of sexuality as originating in childhood seduction to be another kind of attempt to retain its otherness, the uninterpretability of sexuality and hence its irreducibility (see also Stein 1998). But I think it would be more in line with Freud's legacy to keep the irreducibility without shifting to an external source. The otherness of sexuality (according to Freud) is integral to it, not introduced into it.
9 On the one hand, he says that this is in order to keep the instinct within its normal range of expression. On the other, the normal range of expression is determined by what arouses these feelings.
10 One might recall here that Freud speaks in this context (as well as in Dora's case) of the hysteric as one who is disgusted by sexuality. However, it is interesting to see that for Freud in the *Three Essays* what seems to set the hysteric apart from the normal person is not the *disgust* per se, but rather the fact that in contrast to the normal the hysteric lacks a strong sexual instinct that "enjoys overriding this disgust" (Freud 1905: 152).

There may, however, be one true exception to my claim that Freud dismisses evaluation when he considers sexuality from his instinct-centred perspective. At several points in the first of the *Three Essays*, Freud suggests that the *domination* of an aim or practice may justify referring to it as pathological. This occurs when the aim or practice becomes independent of others' aims and practices; it becomes exaggerated and fixed; it becomes the only means to satisfaction, replacing so-called normal aims and practices (e.g. in certain fetishes or sadistic sexual behaviour) (e.g. 1905: 154, 157, 158). It is unclear why the domination of a sexual aim or practice justifies referring to it as pathological. Perhaps one could argue that from an instinctual perspective there is value to diversity, or that domination stands opposed to Freud's pervasive value of recognizing truth. But Freud does not develop such arguments and so this exception remains without reason and out of line with the more general trend of Freud's thinking in regard to the instinct, which does not include any evaluative considerations.

11 Alternatively, one could discard the Oedipus complex. If one has only loving relational wishes which could cause no harm, then one could more readily bracket any evaluation of sexual practices.

References

Blass, R.B. (1992). Did Dora have an Oedipus Complex? A Re-examination of the Theoretical Context of Freud's "Fragment of an Analysis". *The Psychoanalytic Study of the Child* 47, 159–187.

Blass, R.B. (2001). On the Teaching of the Oedipus Complex: On making Freud Meaningful to University Students by Unveiling his Essential Ideas on the Human Condition. *International Journal of Psychoanalysis* 82, 1105–1121.

Blass, R.B. (2006). The Role of Authority in Grounding and Concealing Truth. Special issue: *Truth and Tradition in Psychoanalysis*. *The American Imago* 63, 331–353.

Blass, R.B. & Simon, B. (1994). The Value of the Historical Perspective to Contemporary Psychoanalysis: Freud's "Seduction Hypothesis". *International Journal of Psychoanalysis* 75, 677–694.

Compton, A. (1981). On the Psychoanalytic Theory of Instinctual Drives – II: The Sexual Drives and the Ego Drives. *Psychoanalytic Quarterly* 50, 219–237.

D'Ercole, A. (2014). Be Careful What You Wish For! The Surrender of Gender. *Psychoanalytic Quarterly* 83, 249–279.

Freud, S. (1900). *The Interpretation of Dreams.* J. Strachey (ed.), *Standard Edition 2*. London: Hogarth.

Freud, S. (1905). *Three Essays on the Theory of Sexuality*, *SE 7*.

Freud, S. (1914). On Narcissism, *SE 14*.

Freud, S. (1915). Instincts and Their Vicissitudes, *SE 14*.

Freud, S. (1917a). Mourning and Melancholia, *SE 17*.

Freud, S. (1917b). A Difficulty in the Path of Psychoanalysis, *SE 17*.

Freud, S. (1921). Group Psychology and the Analysis of the Ego, *SE 18*.

Freud, S. (1923). The Ego and the Id, *SE 19*.

Freud–Jung (1974). *The Freud-Jung Letters.* London: The Hogarth Press and Routledge & Kegan Paul.

Gay, P. (1988). *Freud: A Life for Our Time.* New York: Norton.

Green, A. (1995). Has Sexuality Anything to do with Psychoanalysis? *International Journal of Psychoanalysis* 76, 871–883.

Heimann, P.P. (1952). Certain Functions of Introjection and Projection in Early Infancy. In M. Klein, P.P. Heimann, S. Isaacs & J. Riviere (eds.), *Developments in Psychoanalysis*. London: Hogarth, 122–168.

Klein, M. (1952). The Origins of Transference. *International Journal of Psychoanalysis* 33, 433–438.

Kulish, N. & Holtzman, D. (2014). The Widening Scope of Indications for Perversion. *Psychoanalytic Quarterly* 83, 281–313.

Laplanche, J. (1970). *Life and Death in Psychoanalysis.* Baltimore, MD and London: Johns Hopkins University Press.

Laplanche, J. & Pontalis, J.B. (1973). *The Language of Psycho-Analysis.* London: Hogarth.

Laufer, M. (1982). The Formation and Shaping of the Oedipus Complex: Clinical Observations and Assumptions. *International Journal of Psychoanalysis* 63, 217–227.

Moss, D. (2014). Introduction: "The Sexual Aberrations" – Where do we Stand Today? *Psychoanalytic Quarterly* 83, 241–247.

Quinodoz, J.M. (2005). *Reading Freud: A Chronological Exploration of Freud's Writings.* London: Routledge.

Ricoeur, P. (1970). *Freud and Philosophy.* New Haven, CT: Yale University Press.

Scarfone, D. (2014). The *Three Essays* and the Meaning of the Infantile Sexual in Psychoanalysis. *Psychoanalytic Quarterly* 83, 327–344.

Stein, R. (1998). The Enigmatic Dimension of Sexual Experience: The "Otherness" of Sexuality and Primal Seduction. *Psychoanalytic Quarterly* 67, 594–625.

2
FREUD'S DISCUSSION WITH PSYCHIATRY ON SEXUALITY, DRIVES AND OBJECTS IN *THREE ESSAYS*

Herman Westerink

Introduction

Although Freud's 1905 *Three Essays on the Theory of Sexuality* is only a short text in comparison to the voluminous studies on sexuality published by his predecessors in the field of the scientific study of sexuality and the perversions, he considered it to be one of his key publications.[1] We know Freud reissued his text four times, inserting additional material in every new edition. The end result, the 1924 version of *Three Essays*, reflects two decades of developments in psychoanalytic thought. When reading the 1905 edition, one therefore always has to take into account that much of what are considered to be the fundamental psychoanalytic concepts and constructs were not yet defined or even introduced. In 1905, Freud had not yet launched his drive or libido theory, the concept of narcissism, the Oedipus complex, the notion of ambivalence or the developmental stages.

In this chapter, several of the main theoretical and methodological aspects of the text will be highlighted in order to reveal the radicality of the text by exploring its central concepts and the composition of its ideas relative to the contemporary psychiatric literature. The reading of *Three Essays* is guided by the idea that with this text Freud (again) attempted to launch psychoanalysis in the field of psychiatry, opting for a double strategy. On the one hand, he adapts to the conceptual framework of psychiatric reasoning by integrating the key concepts and classifications into his text. On the other, he redefines these concepts from the perspective of his clinical insights in hysteria and in continuity with his own thought that was based in neurophysiology.

In discussion with psychiatry

The opening passages of *Three Essays* reveal Freud's double strategy. On the one hand, he clearly sites his text in the context of a body of thought on sexuality, perversion and pathology established in late nineteenth-century psychiatry and sexology. References to Richard von Krafft-Ebing, Albert Moll, Iwan Bloch and Magnus Hirschfeld, among others, are telling in this respect. The underlying intention is all too obvious: Freud is convinced that psychoanalytic methods and theory will not only make an important contribution to the field but are also the most promising for the further exploration of sexuality in the field. In other words, Freud attempted with this text to launch psychoanalysis in institutionalized psychiatry. In 1906, he makes this intention explicit in a letter to Eugen Bleuler – psychiatrist at Burghölzli, Switzerland – in which he writes the following: "I am confident that we will soon conquer psychiatry" (Borch-Jacobsen & Shamdasani 2012: 59).

On the other hand, Freud immediately points out that his text constitutes a break with the principle and approaches maintained by his predecessors. He presents his text as opposed to "the popular view" and "the poetic fable" (Freud 1905a: 135–136). This fable basically concerns the conceptualization of the sexual drive – more precise, the genital drive (*Geschlechtstrieb*) – as the manifestation of the reproduction instinct (in both human and animal life) in the service of the preservation of the species. In this approach, in which the functionality of the drives and instincts were underscored, sexuality had its analogy in hunger as the expression of the need for ingestion in the service of self-preservation. Indeed, Krafft-Ebing and others had stated in their major writings that sexuality ought to be defined in terms of its natural function in the service of reproduction. This reproduction should not be regarded as the result of individual sexual preferences, but as the necessary and normal expression of a strong natural instinct for the preservation of the mental and physical capacities of the individual (Krafft-Ebing 1903: 1).[2] Sexuality was thus defined in functional terms as a means towards an end. This functional approach not only enabled him to identify normal sexual acts and the normal choice of sexual partners but also to classify the sexual pathologies, i.e. the perversions. The so-called "anomalies of the sexual function" were nothing, but all possible deviations from the norm of reproduction. This was clearly expressed in his definition of perversion: "With opportunity for the natural satisfaction of the sexual instinct, every expression of it that does not correspond with the purpose of nature – i.e., propagation – must be regarded as perverse" (1903: 52–53). It is this criterion of the natural function of the sexual instinct that links the four main perversions to each other. After all, sadism, masochism, fetishism and contrary sexual instincts, i.e. inversion (soon further differentiated into homosexuality, bisexuality, etc.), have no essential features in common except for their non-procreativity. Although Krafft-Ebing in his later writings from around 1900 nuanced the strict implementation of this principle, while turning his attention to psychological aspects of sexuality such as sexual pleasure and the attachment to objects, he never fundamentally questioned his own starting point. Freud's *Three Essays* offer a fundamental critique of this starting point. In the works of Krafft-Ebing and others, Freud identifies a number of other mistaken views on sexuality: it was seen as absent in childhood (since infants cannot be reproductive) and supposedly only first gained momentum in puberty after the sexual organs had come to full maturation. Nevertheless, these authors also paved the way for Freud, who in his *Three Essays*, for example, approves of the basic forms of perversions Krafft-Ebing had listed.

In order to launch psychoanalysis in the field of psychiatry, Freud not only adopts the formal style of the psychiatric literature – and this is visible in the typical layout of the text with the headings in the margins – but also the main conceptual framework. Until 1905, Freud's own conceptual framework, as he had developed it in his studies on hysteria, neurasthenia and anxiety neurosis in the 1890s, mainly revolved around the notions of impulse (*Reiz*), (endogenous) excitation, affect, reflex and resistance – concepts developed from his background in neurophysiology. The concept of *Trieb* had not been part of that framework. It was in *Three Essays* that Freud first elaborates this concept in line with the authors mentioned above who had preferred the word *Trieb* over *Instinkt*. In doing so, Freud simply adopted the key concept par excellence from the literature of his predecessors. Krafft-Ebing, following a Darwinian train of thought, spoke of a *Selbsterhaltungstrieb* and a *Geschlechtstrieb* which he defined in terms of a *Naturtrieb*, i.e. a drive in the service of reproduction human beings share with animals, that can, however, also be sublimated to serve as a source for cultural products. Albert Moll followed Krafft-Ebing in this distinction, reasoning that the concept of *Trieb* should not be used to describe all contingent psychic movements, intentions, strivings and acts of will – as, for example, Wilhelm Wundt had argued – but instead should be used to denote the psychic disposition that pushes a person to perform a certain act. Moll further stated that this is a rather general description that raises an important question, namely that of the distinction between *Trieb* and *Instinkt*. He argued that the *Geschlechtstrieb* – the drive aimed at coitus and intimacy with an adult partner of the opposite sex – is merely the conscious and subjective side of an unconscious *Fortpflanzunsinstinkt* that has reproduction as its goal. Although *Trieb* and *Instinkt* are thus basically interchangeable concepts describing the same process, Moll prefers *Trieb* precisely because of its subjective side, i.e. its relevance for an understanding of the psychological aspects of sexuality such as sexual satisfaction, attachment and object choice. He presents his views on the distinction between instinct and drive as the solution to conceptual problems present in the contemporary literature (Moll 1898: 1–8). Freud – and with him later psychoanalysis – inherits the conceptual problems involved in this literature. We only have to think of the long-lasting debate about how to translate the German word *Trieb* – drive or instinct (Johnston 2005: 156 ff.).

What does Freud tell us about the drives in 1905? First, he argues that the human sexual drive is not naturally organized by an inherent norm or according to some innate functional principle. The sexual drive (*Sexualtrieb*) is not about an innate behavioural pattern with an invariable goal – it is not like Moll's or Krafft-Ebing's heteronormative *Geschlechtstrieb*. The sexual drive is not some form of innate knowledge of what to do or how to act and behave in relation to objects. Freud will make perfectly clear that the sexual drive has no inherent object or aim.

Second, we can learn from Freud's text that he accepts without criticism the Darwinian train of thought of his predecessors that psychic life is characterized by two – and only two – fundamental tendencies: sexuality and self-preservation. In the famous passage on sensual sucking (*Lutschen*), Freud will distinguish between sexual pleasure and satisfaction, on the one hand, and the need for taking nourishment, on the other. He does not speak there of a nutrition drive (or drive for self-preservation), but he does distinguish between the sexual and the non-sexual, associating the latter with hunger and the need for nutrition. Hence, since this sensual sucking seems completely independent from the need for nutrition, according to Freud, we have no choice but to consider it sexual. Freud does not discuss ingestion and self-preservation, but from his scattered remarks we could deduce that self-preservation is very much organized in an instinctual way, that is to say, hunger naturally moves a person to seek nutrition. The drive for self-preservation, as the paradigm of hunger and ingestion shows, is organized in a very functional way. Third, Freud's discussion of the perversions, and his claim that the various perversions show us the building blocks of sexuality, leads him to conclude that "perhaps the sexual instinct [drive] itself may be no simple thing, but put together from components which have come apart again in the perversions" (Freud 1905a: 162). If the sexual activities are composites, maybe the source from which they spring is also something composed. It is from this conclusion that Freud makes the step towards a theory of the polymorphous perverse nature of infantile sexuality, the partial drives and the erogenous zones. Fourth, in discussing these partial drives he writes that these warrant further analysis. He then writes the following sentences that can be seen as his first attempt to define the sexual drive:

> We can distinguish in them (in addition to an "instinct" [drive] which is not sexual and which has its source in motor impulses) a contribution from an organ capable of receiving stimuli (e.g. the skin, the mucous membrane or a sense organ). An organ of this kind will be described in this connection as an "erotogenic zone" – as being the organ whose excitations lends the instinct [drive] a sexual character.
>
> *(1905a: 168)*[3]

These sentences were deleted from the 1915 edition and in this and subsequent editions were replaced by another description that paralleled his drive theory as depicted in "Instincts and Their Vicissitudes" (Freud 1915). The reason for deleting the sentences concerns the reception of the first edition of *Three Essays*; in the aftermath of its publication these sentences had given rise to various interpretations that would prove unacceptable to Freud.[4] Was Freud speaking of one (primal) "drive" or some "drive" (among other drives)? And why use brackets? Was this perhaps because he himself had no clear idea about how to conceptualize *Trieb* relative to *Instinkt* or, as a matter fact, relative to the concepts he had used in past writings to indicate the constant or occasional pressing organic forces on psychic life such as endogenous excitation (*Erregung*), impulse (*Reiz*) or striving (*Strebung*)?

Apparently, redefining sexuality by means of the conceptual framework of the psychiatric literature (instinct and drive), on the one hand, and in line with the neurophysiology-based psychoanalytic theoretical constructs (impulse, stimulus, excitation) produced in the previous years, on the other, constitutes a theoretical problem for Freud – a problem that will also haunt his later writings. It is only in terms of the broader context, i.e. the launching of psychoanalysis in the field of psychiatry by adopting what Arnold Davidson has called a "psychiatric style of reasoning" (Davidson 2001), that we get a clearer picture of what Freud is driving at. He attempts to rethink psychiatric concepts and classifications from the perspective of his own clinical approach and findings. He does so without breaking with either the biological connotations of the psychiatric concepts or the neurophysiological background of his own thought. The drive does not entail an innate programme for object choices and aims, and yet the drive originates from biological sources and proceeds along organic pathways; the pleasure resulting from the drive cathexed to excitable body zones does not originate from individual preferences and is not determined by a cultural realm of possibilities. Seen from this perspective, the *Trieb* still shares important features with the *Instinkt*.[5]

As already suggested in the previous paragraphs, the main distinction in the 1905 *Three Essays* is not the one between drive and instinct, but between the sexual drive (*Sexualtrieb*) and the genital drive (*Geschlechtstrieb*). The sexual drive is used by Freud to conceptualize the autoerotic infantile sexuality. The genital drive is first used to describe the functional – instinctual – theories of sexuality provided by Freud's predecessors. Given his radical critique of the functional heteronormative theories of his predecessors, it is a remarkable and surprising fact that Freud in the third essay – on the transformations in puberty – connects to the reasoning of his predecessors again using the concept of the genital drive to describe what he calls the "final, normal shape" of sexuality, that is to say, the sexuality characterized by the "fact" that "the erogenous zones become subordinated to the primacy of the genital zone", and that the sexual drive "is now subordinated to the reproductive function" (Freud 1905a: 207). In other words, the infantile sexual drive is now shaped into the genital drive in the service of procreation (and consequently the heterosexual object choice is now regarded to be the "normal" form of sexuality). In the next paragraphs we will further explore this distinction between infantile and pubertal (adult) sexuality.

Sexual objects, aims and reaction formations

As already said, Freud makes clear from the very start of his text that he radically rejects the premises and paradigms which his predecessors never fundamentally questioned, despite the fact that their clinical material provided the opportunities for them to do so. He radically inverts the perspective on sexuality that was developed by his predecessors. A theory of sexuality should not start with the identification of normal sexuality in order to define the deviations and distortions, but should, on the contrary, be based on a clinical study of the sexual drive from the perspective of the variety of sexual objects and aims for which the sexual perversions provide evidence. After the dismissal of the contemporary explanations of sexual deviations and after a discussion of inversion (homosexuality), Freud concludes that the relation between the sexual drive and the sexual object needs to be reconsidered: "It seems probable that the sexual instinct [drive] is in the first instance independent of its object; nor is its origin likely to be due to its object's attractions" (1905a: 148). This is a conclusion with far-reaching consequences. The idea that the sexual drive is originally without an object, i.e. that it expresses itself in a non-intersubjective way and does not in any way depend on the presence of an object, is a conclusion that concerns sexuality in general.[6] The discussion of the sexual aim is developed along similar lines. According to Freud, the observation of sexual activities and relationships shows that the sexual aim is hardly ever limited to the genitals but involves the whole body as a surface of excitation and pleasure. It is not without irony and a sense for provocation that he mentions kissing (defined by Freud as the contact between the mucous membrane of the lips that constitute the entrance to the digestive tract) as a perverse act generally regarded to be an aspect of every normal sexual relationship and therefore held in great esteem in civilized societies. Kissing is a perverse act just like oral-genital activities, anal-genital activities and so forth. After all, in all these activities parts of the body are involved that do not belong to the sexual apparatus *strictu sensu*. He adds that the various sexual activities express a certain general human need for variation (*Bedürfnis nach Variation*) – a remark deleted from the 1920 edition onwards (Freud 1905b: 13). One question immediately arises: why is it that certain perverse acts are held in great esteem, while others can be classified as clearly abnormal? Is this just a matter of cultural convention, or is there perhaps another dynamic at work?

In 1905, Freud argues that this need for variation collides with cultural conventions on normal and abnormal sexual activities. It leads Freud to make some notes on the relation between organic processes and cultural prohibitions. Drawing upon his studies of hysteria, he writes that shame and disgust are to be regarded as reaction formations. These reaction formations are psychic counter forces that are spontaneously constructed in order to repress the displeasure that somehow results from sexual excitation. The crucial point here is that shame and disgust are seen as the organically determined (*organisch bedingte*) limitation of the sexual drive without the involvement of external objects, norms and principles. Shame and disgust are therefore not the earliest manifestations of internalized cultural morality. The relation between the two is actually the other way around: cultural morality can only follow and impress "somewhat more clearly and deeply" the psychic lines "which have already been laid down organically" (Freud 1905a: 177–178). Culture is inscribed in already existing psychic patterns and dams and is thus not the "radical other" of nature opposing and checking blind natural tendencies. But culture is also not the concrete regulation founded upon a natural organization of sexuality relative to a normal object or aim. After 1905, Freud seems to change his position when he starts to put to the fore the notion of cultural development and to argue that sexual drive is subjected to historical processes, i.e. that in primitive societies sexual drive is free and without a specific object and aim, whereas in later cultural stages sexual drive is solely used for reproduction (Freud 1908). One wonders whether Freud's later articulation of developmental stages in the life of the individual is not in fact derived from his ideas on cultural development that very much mirror the mentality of his time: maybe there is no natural law that governs sexuality, but at least there is the gradual advancement of civilization that provides us with a norm. This idea is not yet present in the 1905 *Three Essays*.

The conclusion one has to draw from the first essay and Freud's views on the perverse polymorphous nature of infantile sexuality is already foreshadowed in his elaborations of the sexual aim: strictly speaking there are no perversions, since what were previously called the perversions are in fact merely sexual activities consistent with the sexual disposition original to all human beings. There is a variety of perverse acts, but there are no perversions in the sense in which Krafft-Ebing defined them, namely as neuropathic dispositions grounding a specific identity to be distinguished from normal sexual life.

So why is kissing acceptable whereas other perverse acts (such as licking shit) are not? Freud does not provide a clear answer to this question, but two important aspects of the text provide us with important clues. First, the fact that Freud takes hysteria as the model for the study of sexuality implies highlighting the hysteric's disgust of excrement and the strong reaction formations relative to the anal function. Second, Freud's account of sexuality as pleasure discovered while sucking the breast immediately links pleasurable sensations experienced at the lips to an acceptable – even necessary – act. In short, for (most) infants, kissing is pleasurable and does not evoke the strong reaction formation of disgust one finds with regard to excrement. Cultural conventions connect to these reaction formations.

Understanding sexuality: hysteria is a model

In *Three Essays*, Freud engages in the discussion with psychiatric literature from the perspective of his own clinical practice, more specifically, from the perspective of hysteria (Freud 1905a: 163). We know that the first major theory on the aetiology of hysteria – the seduction theory – was still formulated in line with the general approach of his predecessors. In this theory, which was developed in the mid-1890s, the neuroses were regarded as a deviation from "normality" because they originated from an "abnormal" (traumatic) moment in early childhood. When Freud started to question these accidental influences, he eventually concluded that neither hysteria nor perversion result from abnormal neuropathic dispositions or abnormal traumatic moments, but from a general human sexual disposition (Freud 1906). Among other things, this called for a redefinition of the relation between pathology and normality, and Freud provided this with the idea that pathologies can be seen as exaggerations and intensifications of normal sexual impulses and acts. For this reason, the model in *Three Essays* is hysteria. In hysteria we find constitutionally higher-than-average sexual energy and also we find repression of sexual impulses "in excess of the normal quantity". Hence, hysteria is a pathology "at least approximate" to normality, Freud claims, and at the same time it is characterized by higher-than-average quantities of sexual energy, by intensified and excessive repression and by corporeal symptom formations that appear to be magnifications of normal corporeal expressions of the always more or less unstable human emotional life (Freud 1905a: 163–164). For these reasons, hysteria presents itself as suitable for an anthropological approach to sexuality and hence to human nature as such (Van Haute 2005; Van Haute & Geyskens 2012).

What, then, is sexuality when its model is hysteria? According to Freud, the hysterical constitution highlights three central aspects of sexuality. First, there is the bisexual disposition. Yet, in spite of the fact that he originally intended to give his text on the theory of sexuality the title *Die menschliche Bisexualität* (Freud 1985: 448), Freud does not provide a comprehensive theory of bisexuality in *Three Essays*. Second, there are the tendencies to every kind of anatomical extension of sexual activity which one finds in hysteria more often and more intensely in comparison with normal sexuality (Freud 1905a: 165). The hysteric's symptom formations always indicated an inclination towards the oral or anal erogenous zones that produced pleasure in early childhood and were then repressed through disgust and shame. Third, in this same context, Freud develops the idea that human sexuality has to overcome its initial mixing with excremental functions. This idea is developed in detail in his text on Dora that was also published in 1905 (Freud 1905c: 31).[7]

Hysteria provides insights into the human sexual disposition and thus into human nature as such. Yet, the model of hysteria inevitably comes with limitations. If the central dynamics – the "complex" – of hysteria concern bisexuality, the excitable erogenous zones, pleasure and disgust, then we can also identify a number of issues that do not as such constitute a key problem in hysteria (which does not imply that such issues are completely absent). Based on popular opinions in Freudian scholarship, one of the issues we might have expected to play a role in the text would be the relation between the infant and the parents, notably the father figure, or, in other words, we might have expected some version of an Oedipus complex or at least hints in that direction. There are several reasons why this is not the case. We know of course that Freud in his earlier views on hysteria focused on the traumatic origin of psychopathologies and highlighted the role of the seducer – most often the father. In 1905, he argues that he never exaggerated the frequency and importance of traumatizing seduction in early infancy, but he adds: "I consequently overrated the importance of seduction in comparison with the factors of sexual constitution and development" (Freud 1905a: 190). In other words, Freud did not abandon the central hypothesis of the seduction theory and the central role of the parental figures in that theory as such, but he shifts his attention to the general human sexual constitution as the main factor in the aetiology of the psychopathologies. Seduction is still traumatic, says Freud, since it confronts the infant with a sexual object at a period in life in which it is neither physically nor mentally prepared to deal with an adult object-related sexuality. But hysteria should be understood from constitutional factors, not from accidental factors and the premature confrontation with sexual objects. In fact, Freud shows in the Dora case that certain events only acquire a traumatic status when a hysteric disposition is activated and expressed in the event. Trauma follows disposition. From this we can understand why Freud never developed the theory of the Oedipus complex while taking hysteria as the *primus inter pares* among the psychopathologies: when infantile sexuality is auto-erotic and without object, it hardly makes sense to develop a theory in which object relations between the infant and parents are the key to understanding the infant's sexual life. In the aetiology of hysteria, the object relations, as such, are not decisive. It is only after Freud writes the case study of Little Hans as the clinical case that should convince his opponents of his views on infantile sexuality that he feels forced to make some important adjustments. In 1910, he adds a footnote to the text in which he writes that a distinction between infantile sexuality characterized by auto-erotism, on the one hand, and the later changes in puberty when sexuality becomes object-related, on the other, cannot be maintained, because early infants – like Little Hans – are already capable of an object choice (1905a: 193–194). One might say that by expressing the idea that in infantile sexuality a tendency towards an object can be identified, this statement eventually gives rise to an oedipal perspective on sexuality. In the course of this development, the seduction and trauma theory Freud still defended in 1905 is further put into perspective.[8]

Another important problem for Freud is aggression. In hysteria, aggression is apparently not part of the key complex. That is to say, in his various studies of hysteria Freud does mention rage and anger, but not sadism or masochism. It is exactly the latter phenomena that are listed by Krafft-Ebing among the main perversions. Seen from the perspective of infantile sexuality as characterized by autoerotic pleasure, finding pleasure in aggression and cruelty are difficult to explain. Freud will reason that aggression in sexuality can only be explained with reference to a source other than the erogenous zones. He therefore introduces the concept of a drive for mastery and argues that the alliance between aggression and sexuality is established relatively late in childhood (1905a: 157 ff.). Nevertheless, the problem of the origin and nature of aggression is a pressing issue. This is one of the reasons why Freud will turn his attention from hysteria to obsessional neurosis in the years after the first edition of *Three Essays*. After all, in obsessional neurosis one can most clearly witness the ambivalent feelings towards objects, i.e. the sadistic impulses towards love objects.[9]

Yet another problem concerns fetishism. In a remark deleted from the later editions of *Three Essays*, Freud notes the following: "Among the unconscious trains of thought found in the neuroses there is nothing corresponding to a tendency to fetishism" (1905a: 167). Consequently, hysteria does not seem to provide an adequate model for understanding this perversion. Apparently, the relation between the neuroses and perversions is a bit more complex than Freud suggests in his well-known dictum that "the neuroses are, so to say, the negative of the perversions" (1905a: 165).

Sexuality as autoerotic pleasure

In the second essay Freud addresses the question of the origin and nature of sexuality in a section on the autoerotic manifestations of infantile sexuality (1905a: 179 ff.).[10]

The starting point and model for his discussion of these manifestations is the phenomenon of *Lutschen*, a rhythmic oral activity that he describes as a sexual activity. Why and in what sense is this sensual sucking sexual? Freud observes that sucking is pleasurable and "leads either to sleep or even to a motor reaction in the nature of an orgasm" (1905a: 179–180). Freud's main point is that this pleasure is sexual because it is essentially autoerotic and non-functional. It has indeed nothing to do with the drive for nourishment and hence it is not related to self-preservation, the need for food or the satisfaction of hunger. Freud here mainly applies his basic Darwinian scheme that whatever is not related to self-preservation is *for that very reason* sexual. Nevertheless, Freud says that there is a primal activity that triggers sensual sucking, and this activity is breast-sucking. At first sight, it might appear as if sensual sucking therefore does depend on the presence or absence of a specific object, but this is strictly speaking not the case. The breast, or as a matter of fact one of its surrogates such as a milk bottle, is the only means by which the infant discovers that sucking is pleasurable. Or, more concretely, while sucking at the mother's breast, the lips of the infant behave as an erogenous zone and the warm milk creates a pleasurable excitation that the infant will later try to reproduce. This implies that the relation to the breast or, as a matter of fact the attachment to the object providing the milk is not essential to sexuality. Breasts or bottles are only instrumental in the discovery of autoerotic pleasure. The paradigm for infantile sexuality, Freud writes, is the lips kissing themselves, not the actual or phantasmatic attachment to an object and also not the excitation of the genitals as Freud will later suggest in other writings. In infantile sexuality, kissing is not aimed at connecting to an object, but at the pleasurable sensation of the lips being touched.

At least this is what Freud says in the first two essays. In the third essay seemingly contradictory statements can be identified. Finding the object (*Objektfinding*) in puberty, Freud claims, is actually nothing but re-finding it (*Wiederfindung*) (1905a: 222). Does this statement not clearly express that there is already a sexual object in early childhood that is re-found in puberty and adult sexual life? The statement, however, only seemingly contradicts what Freud said in the first two essays. It is only in puberty that sexuality gets directed towards objects. From then on, the erogenous zones are reinvested from the perspective of adult object-related sexuality. The breast gets a new meaning in this process. Whereas it was merely the thing by which the infant first experiences autoerotic pleasure through the rhythmic sucking, the sensation of warm milk on the lips and in the mouth, etc., the breast is now part of the object (person) that makes the experience of pleasure possible. This person is also capable of experiencing pleasure herself/himself – the latter now becoming a new aim in sexual activity as well. In other words, it is only now that breast-sucking and the breast get a new status in sexual activities and fantasies.

The idea that finding the object is inevitably re-finding it has been very dominant in the post-Freudian psychoanalytic theories. In particular, the idea of an irreducible difference between the object we find and the object we have lost has been used to defend the idea that drive and desire in Freud originate in negativity – we can find this idea in all object-relational schools, from Winnicott to Lacan. It is precisely this structural difference between the lost (or lacking) and the re-found object that would be the motor of psychic life. However, what we lost is, according to Freud, not an object but a specific regime of autoerotic pleasure. Negativity (loss or lack) does not play any role in his conceptualization of sexuality as pleasure. On the contrary, the drive is a force that originates from an organic source, is cathexed to erogenous zones, finds pleasure in the release of tension and meets its inner limitation in the reaction formations of shame and disgust. The dynamics of loss and desire are later mainly elaborated in his views on melancholy, and it is this theory of melancholy (and depression) that becomes paradigmatic for the view of psychic life in many post-Freudian theories.

Puberty, object relations and the reorganization of pleasure

In *Three Essays*, Freud does not follow a developmental approach. He merely distinguishes infantile autoerotic sexuality from puberty and the reorganization of sexuality. In the third essay, Freud devotes his attention to the structural changes that occur at the beginning of puberty. It is only at the beginning of puberty that the genital zone becomes the predominant one – the lips apparently lose their paradigmatic status (1905a: 207). Nothing in his text thus far obliged him to give a privileged theoretical status to this choice. It is unclear why we should give any privilege to the genital zone as such. Puberty is also the period in which the sexual difference between man and woman is first established. Freud does not mean to say that the infant cannot make a distinction between a man (father, brother, etc.) and a woman (mother, sister, etc.); his point is rather that it is only in puberty that this distinction is related to sexuality. The reorganization of sexuality in terms of object relations equals the reorganization of sexuality in terms of object choices relative to sexual difference. This is why Freud can state that the object choice – in most cases this will be the heterosexual object choice – builds on the fact that objects had always been present in the individual's life. That is to say, the object choices develop along the lines of the already established tender relationships towards the caregivers, primarily the parents. But it is only in puberty that these objects can become sexual objects. Why the object of the genital drive should be a heterosexual one remains an unsolved question. After all, in the first essay, Freud had denied an inherent object and aim of the sexual drive. In his discussion of sexuality in puberty, however, Freud in a sense returns to the functional approach of the predecessors he had so severely criticized and does so without providing arguments. Apparently, Freud has difficulties with accepting the radical consequences of his approach. One consequence of his ideas on infantile sexuality would have been to say that the object choice is guided by the notion of pleasure, and not by sexual difference, the primacy of the genitals or the aim of reproduction. The underlying problem seems to be the following: Freud's conceptualization of infantile sexuality is largely done within a biomedical framework in which inherent objects and aims are dismissed. The reorganization of sexuality in puberty is clearly situated in a cultural context of family structures, incest taboos and a larger social environment. This is exactly the point that Freud will further develop in his early cultural writings; perhaps adult sexuality is not organized according to innate patterns, but is organized according to the logics of advanced cultures, which means that sexuality is organized in the service of procreation after all. The step from infantile sexuality to the reorganization in puberty is by and large the step from a biomedical perspective towards a theory that takes the cultural and moral context into account. It is only in *Totem and Taboo* that Freud will first present a model for the transition from pre-cultural family life, via primitive societies, to the more advanced social and moral structures in civilized societies (Freud 1912–13).

The disappearance of hysteria and the turn to the object

Notably in the editions of *Three Essays* from 1915 and 1920, Freud introduces large paragraphs that contain important new theoretical insights gained after 1905. Occasionally, sentences and notions from the 1905 edition are deleted and/or reformulated – we have already come across some examples. Within the limited possibilities of this chapter it is impossible to discuss all such changes and additions extensively or to point out all the theoretical problems that arise with the insertion of new material. Two important issues should be highlighted, however, in order to provide context for the later insertions.

First, there are major shifts in psychiatry that force Freud to change his perspective. We have said that Freud takes hysteria as a model for the theory of sexuality and the perversions. The adoption of this perspective is hardly surprising given the fact that hysteria had been at the centre of his clinical practice and theoretical considerations from the time he went to Paris to study hysteria with Jean-Martin Charcot until the publication of the Dora case and the *Three Essays*. These two publications would in fact prove to be the last great texts on hysteria. After 1905, Freud scarcely writes about hysteria, and sometimes he does so only to argue that what he had formerly identified as hysteria should actually be considered as another psychopathology (Freud 1923). Hysteria disappears almost overnight from Freud's writings. Why? The answer is related to the very fact that Freud attempts to launch psychoanalysis in the field of psychiatry. It is in this field that the Charcotian hysteria on which Freud's studies of hysteria were based was always considered to be problematic, as its clinical profile was apparently different from the hysteria found in Germany. This is one aspect of an important development that takes place in early twentieth-century psychiatry, a development identified by Mark Micale as "the disappearance of hysteria" from the main psychiatric handbooks such as the various editions of Emil Kraepelin's *Lehrbuch* (Micale 1993, 1995). A year after Freud's remark to Bleuler that they together would conquer psychiatry, Bleuler's colleague Carl Gustav Jung published a book on dementia praecox (Jung 1907) in which many of the symptoms formerly ascribed to hysteria are now reinterpreted in terms of dementia praecox. Not long afterwards, Bleuler himself introduced the concept of schizophrenia, his theories of which were strongly influenced by Freud (Bleuler 1911). In short, the psychoses are deemed to be the most promising field for further developing psychoanalytic theory and for launching psychoanalysis in the field of psychiatry. Freud's text on the case of Schreber from 1911 is the main result of the extensive debate on the psychoses with Jung and others.

The study of the psychoses confronted Freud with a problem that he had not yet been able to identify as such. The problem was the fact that the psychoses made clear that both the object and the ego from which the object choice and relation proceed can be lost in the course of our existence. Adult object relations are not self-evident. In *Three Essays* this had not been an issue. Freud had focused on the conceptualization of infantile sexuality, and the reorganization of sexuality in puberty in terms of adult object-related sexuality was simply taken for granted. The notion of the reproduction instinct had served as a guiding principle here and seemed to provide enough ground not to further problematize the turn to the object. Freud was challenged to consider this issue. The main theoretical concept introduced in the course of his study of psychoses is the concept of narcissism, described by Freud as a stage between autoerotism and object choice in which the infant takes his or her own body as the love object. This connects to what we have already said about the case of Little Hans; infantile sexuality is no longer strictly autoerotic and "without object", but should be seen as naturally developing into object choice. Hence, with narcissism comes the idea of developmental stages and consequently the developmental perspective on sexuality that replaces the earlier model of two relatively separate organizations of sexuality, one in early childhood and one in puberty. The theory of infantile sexuality and the reorganization in puberty is from now on situated in a temporal sequence of stages. This is clearly evidenced by the paragraphs on developmental stages and genital organization inserted in the 1915 edition. The idea that object choice takes place already in infantile sexuality implies that the problematics of the homosexual and heterosexual object choice become more prominent, and indeed in the years after 1905 Freud shows a keen interest in the dynamics of homosexuality (Schreber, Leonardo, narcissism theory).

Psychosis is not the only field that interests Freud. The other psychopathology he turns his attention to is the obsessional neurosis. Like the turn to dementia praecox, this interest in obsessional neurosis can be situated in the context of the disappearance of hysteria and related trends in psychiatry (May-Tolzmann 1998). Obsessional neurosis was not mentioned in the psychiatric literature from the 1890s, but there had been an increasing interest in obsessional ideas (notably in the writings of Westphal, Krafft-Ebing, Kraepelin and Löwenfeld) as familiar with, and yet distinct from, delusional ideas. Freud's introduction of the concept of obsessional neurosis in 1895 and his intensified interest in this particular neurosis after 1905 can thus be seen as part of a larger trend in psychiatry regarding the debate on the relation between neurosis and psychosis.

At least two other factors led him to put this neurosis at the centre of his further theoretical considerations. First, there is the issue already addressed in *Three Essays*, namely that of a certain continuity between the infant's tender feelings (*Zärtlichkeit*) for its primary caregivers and the later sexual object choices it will make. Second, there is the already addressed problem of aggression and cruelty (*Grausamkeit*) in infantile sexuality that needs further clinical and theoretical investigation and conceptualization. In his study of obsessional neurosis, notably in his case study of the Rat Man (Freud 1909), Freud will relate *Zärtlichkeit* and *Grausamkeit* to each other (ambivalence of feelings), to the theory of the drives (sadistic component of the sexual drive) and to the parental figures and substitute object choices (father complex). From this he will develop the Oedipus complex, a complex of associated psychic aspects and mechanisms such as love and hate, guilt, identification, object choice and conscience formation which from 1913 onwards, is going to be identified as the nuclear complex of all the psychoneuroses. Obsessional neurosis thus becomes the main model for understanding the vicissitudes of the drives relative to the problem of aggression, object choices and identifications. It is the final blow to the paradigmatic status of hysteria that had thus far determined his theories. Central aspects of hysteria, such as disgust or bisexuality lose importance, whereas concepts such as the ambivalence of feelings, narcissism, object relations and psychic development become predominant. From that moment onwards, the Oedipus complex is identified as the nuclear complex of all the psychoneuroses, including hysteria, and much of Freud's early, non-oedipal theory of sexuality becomes buried under new theoretical layers.

Notes

1 For a more extensive commentary on the 1905 version of Freud's *Three Essays*, see Van Haute and Westerink (2015 and 2016).
2 On Krafft-Ebing, the sexual instinct and his influence on Freud, see Oosterhuis (2000, 2012) and Davidson (2001). See also Harry Oosterhuis' contribution in this volume.
3 "Neben einem an sich nicht sexuellen, aus motorische Impulsquellen stammenden 'Trieb' unterscheidet man an ihnen einen Beitrag von einem Reize annehmenden Organ (Haut, Schleimhaut, Sinnesorgan). Letzteres soll hier als erogenen Zone bezeichnet werden, als jenes Organ, dessen Erregung dem Trieb den sexuellen Charakter verleiht" (Freud 1905b: 26).
4 The most important came from Jung who argued that Freud suggests a single primordial drive splitting up in various directions causing certain bodily functions, zones and objects to be cathexed with sexuality. In this way, zones (for example, the lips) that were initially without sexual function could receive such a function (kissing) in the context of a natural process of efficient differentiation and growth. In this reading the drive does not become sexual through the link with bodily zones, but, on the contrary, certain bodily zones receive a sexual function when the primordial libido (*Urlibido*) differentiates into various domains and specialized functions. See Patrick Vandermeersch's contribution in this volume.
5 There are other factors that underscore the close relation between *Trieb* and *Instinkt*. As we will see, the sexual pleasure is discovered through ingestion, that is to say, as the side effect of an instinctual organized activity. We should also bear in mind that the reaction formations are defined as organically determined limitations of the drives.
6 The implication is what Arnold Davidson has rightfully described as "a conceptually devastating blow to the entire structure of nineteenth century theories of sexual psychopathology" (Davidson 2001: 79).

7 Freud adds in a footnote: "It is scarcely possible to exaggerate the pathogenic significance of the comprehensive tie uniting the sexual and the excremental, a tie which is at the basis of a very large number of hysterical phobias" (Freud 1905c: 32).
8 If the infant is already capable of object choice, it is difficult to maintain that the child is both physically and mentally not prepared to deal with at least certain aspects of adult object-related sexuality. A key aspect of the seduction theory is thus nuanced.
9 See Jens De Vleminck's contribution in this volume.
10 On this issue see also Geyskens (2005).

References

Bleuler, E. (1911). *Dementia praecox oder Gruppe der Schizophrenien*. Leipzig and Vienna: Deuticke.
Borch-Jacobsen, M. & Shamdasani, S. (2012). *The Freud Files: An Inquiry into the History of Psychoanalysis*. Cambridge, MA: Cambridge University Press.
Davidson, A.I. (2001). *The Emergence of Sexuality: Historical Epistemology and the Formation of Concepts*. Cambridge, MA: Harvard University Press.
Freud, S. (1905a). Three Essays on the Theory of Sexuality. Strachey, J. (ed.), *Standard Edition 7*. London: Hogarth.
Freud, S. (1905b). *Drei Abhandlungen zur Sexualtheorie*. Leipzig and Vienna: Deuticke.
Freud, S. (1905c). Fragment of an Analysis of a Case of Hysteria, *SE 7*.
Freud, S. (1906). My Views on the Part played by Sexuality in the Aetiology of the Neuroses, *SE 7*.
Freud, S. (1908). "Civilized" Sexual Morality and Modern Nervous Illness, *SE 9*.
Freud, S. (1909). Notes upon a Case of Obsessional Neurosis. *SE 10*.
Freud, S. (1911). Psycho-Analytic Notes upon an Autobiographical Account of a Case of Paranoia (Dementia paranoides), *SE 12*.
Freud, S. (1912–13). Totem and Taboo, *SE 13*.
Freud, S. (1915). Instincts and Their Vicissitudes, *SE 14*.
Freud, S. (1923). A Seventeenth-Century Demonological Neurosis, *SE 19*.
Freud, S. (1985). *The Complete Letters of Sigmund Freud to Wilhelm Fliess 1887–1904*. J.M. Masson (ed.), Cambridge, MA and London: Harvard University Press.
Geyskens, T. (2005). *Our Original Scenes: Freud's theory of Sexuality*. Leuven: University Press.
Johnston, A. (2005). *Time Driven: Metapsychology and the Splitting of the Drive*. Evanston, IL: Northwestern University Press.
Jung, C.G. (1907). *Uber die Psychologie der Dementia Praecox: Ein Versuch*. Halle: Verlagsbuchhandlung Carl Marhold.
Krafft-Ebing, R. von (1903). *Psychopathia Sexualis, With Especial Reference to the Antipathic Sexual Instinct: A Medico-Forensic Study*. Transl. F.E. Klaf, New York: Arcade, 1965.
May-Tolzmann, U. (1998). "Obsessional Neurosis": A Nosographic Innovation by Freud. *History of Psychiatry* 9:3, 335–353.
Micale, M. (1993). On the "Disappearance" of Hysteria: A Study in the Clinical Deconstruction of a Diagnosis. *Isis* 84:3, 496–526.
Micale, M. (1995). *Approaching Hysteria: Disease and Its Interpretation*. Princeton, NJ: Princeton University Press.
Moll, A. (1898). *Untersuchungen über die Libido sexualis*, Band 1. Berlin: Fischer.
Oosterhuis, H. (2000). *Stepchildren of Nature: Krafft-Ebing, Psychiatry, and the Making of Sexual Identity*. Chicago, IL: University of Chicago Press.

Oosterhuis, H. (2012). Sexual Modernity in the Works of Richard von Krafft-Ebing and Albert Moll. *Medical History* 56:2, 133–155.

Van Haute, P. (2005). Psychoanalysis and/as Philosophy: The Anthropological Significance of Pathology in Freud's *Three Essays on the Theory of Sexuality* and in the Psychoanalytic Tradition. *Natureza Humana* 7:2, 359–374.

Van Haute, P. & Geyskens, T. (2012). *A Non-Oedipal Psychoanalysis? A Clinical Anthropology of Hysteria in the Work of Freud and Lacan.* Leuven: Leuven University Press.

Van Haute, P. & Westerink, H. (2015). Hysterie, Sexualität und Psychiatrie: Eine Relektüre der ersten Ausgabe der *Drei Abhandlungen zur Sexualtheorie*. In S. Freud, *Drei Abhandlungen zur Sexualtheorie (1905)*. P. Van Haute, C. Huber & H. Westerink (eds.). Vienna: Vienna University Press, 9–56.

Van Haute, P & Westerink, H. (2016). Hysteria, Sexuality and the Deconstruction of Normativity – Rereading Freud's 1905 Edition of Three Essays on the Theory of Sexuality – The 1905 Edition. Transl. K. Kristner, London and New York: Verso, xiii–lxxv

3

THE PRE-FREUDIAN MODERNIZATION OF SEXUALITY

Richard von Krafft-Ebing and Albert Moll

Harry Oosterhuis

Sigmund Freud's general perspective on sexuality and that articulated in his *Three Essays on the Theory of Sexuality* in particular should not be considered as a unique and revolutionary breakthrough, but as part of a broader development: the modernization of sexuality. A new understanding of sexuality began to take shape in the last two decades of the nineteenth century, which in turn came about against the background of wider historical developments. The conceptual groundwork was laid by some psychiatrists, in particular Richard von Krafft-Ebing (1840–1902) and Albert Moll (1862–1939). Their pioneering role has largely been forgotten, ignored or belittled, and their work has often been presented in a simplistic way. Therefore, I will stress the continuing historical relevance of their work.[1]

Traditionally, sexuality had been mainly understood in moral-religious and legal terms, either as virtuous or as sinful and criminal *behaviour*. The new psychiatric interest in sexuality was linked to forensic medicine that focused on criminal acts like rape, sodomy and public indecency. Whereas physicians first argued that mental and nervous disorders *resulted* from improper sexual conduct, psychiatrists suggested that they were the *cause* of deviance. In many cases, they added, such behaviour should not be regarded as sinful or criminal, but as symptomatic of a pathology. From around 1870 onward, under the influence of evolutionary and degeneration theory, psychiatrists shifted the focus from immoral acts to an innate morbid condition and the personal characteristics of moral offenders, who should be treated as patients rather than punished as sinners or criminals. Collecting and publishing more and more case histories, they diagnosed, categorized, labelled, discussed and explained a wide range of perversions such as uranism, contrary sexual feeling, inversion, homo- and heterosexuality, exhibitionism, voyeurism, fetishism, paedophilia, sadism and masochism. Against this background both Krafft-Ebing and Moll articulated a new perspective, not only on perversion, but also on sexuality in general. What was initiated by Krafft-Ebing in the mid-1880s and elaborated by Moll in the 1890s was a shift from a psychiatric approach in which deviant sexuality was explained as a derived and episodic symptom of a more fundamental mental disorder to a consideration of perversion as an integral part of an autonomous and continuous sexual instinct which deeply affected one's inner self and manifested itself in various forms.

As a professor at the universities of Graz (1872–1889) and Vienna (1889–1902) and working in many fields of psychiatry, Krafft-Ebing was one of the most prominent psychiatrists in Central Europe and a leading forensic expert. As one of the founding fathers of medical sexology he is remembered nowadays chiefly as the author of the bestselling *Psychopathia sexualis* and other works on sexual pathology (Krafft-Ebing 1877, 1886, 1887, 1890, 1901a, 1901b). By naming and classifying virtually all non-procreative sexuality, he synthesized the new psychiatric knowledge about perversion.

Moll ran a private practice in Berlin as a neurologist and psychotherapist between 1887 and 1938, and he established himself as an expert in forensic psychiatry, therapeutic hypnosis and suggestion as well as medical ethics. In 1913 he founded the International Society for Sexual Research, and in 1926 he organized the International Congress for Sexology in Berlin. His main works on sexuality are *Die Conträre Sexualempfindung*; *Das Sexualleben des Kindes* and in particular *Untersuchungen über die Libido sexualis* (Moll 1891, 1897–1898, 1908). The last work offered the most comprehensive and sophisticated theory of sexuality before Freud published the first edition of his *Three Essays* (Freud 1905). Moll, who also edited the *Handbuch der Sexualwissenschaften: Mit besonderer Berücksichtigung der kulturgeschichtlichen Beziehungen* (Moll 1912), arrived at several insights about sexuality that would later be claimed by Freud and his followers to be their own discoveries.

Krafft-Ebing and Moll were in touch with each other and exchanged case histories and opinions. Whereas Krafft-Ebing's work was largely an empirical collection of clinical observations and case studies, and his explanatory comments were rather fragmentary, Moll elaborated many of Krafft-Ebing's thoughts and devised a more systematic theory. Both criticized the criminalization of sexual deviance, in particular homosexuality. Both also showed some appreciation for Freud's early work. Krafft-Ebing, for example, actively supported Freud's application for a teaching-position at the University of Vienna. Nevertheless, both men also shared similar criticisms of Freud. Krafft-Ebing dismissed Freud's early seduction theory as 'a fairy-tale'. According to Moll, Freud distorted his case histories and his patient's dreams in order to make them fit his theories, which, in Moll's view, were strongly coloured by Freud's subjective preoccupations. The way Freud responded to Moll's criticism, by degrading Moll's personality and accomplishments, is certainly one of the less edifying episodes in the history of the psychoanalytic movement. For example, Freud's claim that he was the first to recognize the significance of infantile sexuality and his accusation that Moll had plagiarized him on this subject were groundless.

One of the reasons why psychoanalysis eventually overshadowed the contributions of Krafft-Ebing, Moll and others such as Iwan Bloch and Havelock Ellis was that Freud developed a comprehensive theory, established a therapeutic school, acquired dedicated followers and organized a movement employing disciplinary mechanisms to maintain unity and orthodoxy. Krafft-Ebing did not develop a coherent theory which could be adopted by students or followers. Moll did to some extent, and in the early twentieth century he was a leading medical expert on sexuality, but he was a self-willed and even obstinate character, who did not teach at the university and also lacked any other institutional framework through which to attract students or followers.

A significant similarity in Krafft-Ebing's and Moll's work is the prominent role of so-called 'perverts' as patients, correspondents and informants. Their work is full of case histories, which included many (auto-)biographical accounts, letters and intimate confessions. Both Krafft-Ebing and Moll relied on the experiences and self-descriptions of their clients as an empirical basis for their considerations. By publishing and quoting from letters and autobiographical accounts, they enabled voices to be heard that were usually silenced. Because they argued against traditional condemnations of sexual deviance as sin and crime, individuals approached them in search of understanding and support. Many middle and upper-class men contacted them of their own accord as private patients or corresponded with them in order to explain themselves. In sharing their views in this way with Krafft-Ebing and Moll, these men were given ample opportunity to speak for themselves. Several clients took advantage of the psychiatric approach for their own purposes, to justify themselves, to develop a dialogue about their condition and to criticize the condemnation of their sexual desires as criminal or pathological. It is striking that Krafft-Ebing and Moll did not force these views into the straitjacket of established medical explanations. As more and more clients came up with stories that did not smoothly fit the current moral and medical judgements, Krafft-Ebing's and Moll's approaches increasingly fluctuated between the explanation of perversion in terms of pathology and the recognition of the diversity of sexuality. Like Freud's ongoing theoretical elaborations on sexuality, Krafft-Ebing's and Moll's approach was far from univocal, but full of contradictions and ambiguities.

Against this background of interaction between Krafft-Ebing and Moll as experts on perversion and their articulate clients, the foundation was laid for a fundamental transformation of the definition and explanation of sexuality and of its meaning in human life. There are five outstanding features of sexual modernity that can be found in Krafft-Ebing's and Moll's work, and that foreshadow Freud's approach. The first concerns the conceptualization of sexuality as an inevitable and powerful natural force in human life. The second is the classification of perversions and their relation to 'normal' sexuality. The third relates to the psychological understanding of sexuality. The fourth centres on the close connection between sexuality and personal identity. And the fifth refers to the shift from the reproductive norm to the pleasure of sexuality as well as its relational dimension. All five of these features imply that the modern experience of sexuality is permeated with ambiguities and problems. In the remainder of this chapter I will elaborate on these five features.

Sexuality as an inevitable, natural force

While transferring sexuality from the realm of sin and crime to the domain of health and illness, Krafft-Ebing and Moll made clear that the sexual instinct, as a powerful and compulsive force, was an essential part of human nature. This is the steam engine or pressure-cooker model of the sexual drive; it is viewed as a continuous building up of psychophysical energy, as an irresistible inner pressure that relentlessly seeks release, whatever its object might be (another person, a body part, a fetishist object or a particular scenario).

Closely connected to this model is the Janus-face of sexuality as a highly complex force that is both wholesome and dangerous, and with which everybody has to come to terms. On the one hand, they underlined the then current idea that the sexual urge posed a persistent threat to the moral and social order because of its barely controllable and sometimes explosive, destructive and bizarre nature. Worrisome, for instance, was Krafft-Ebing's claim that the sexual relation between man and woman was rooted in sadomasochism and evoked associations with rape, murder for lust and even cannibalism.

On the other, Krafft-Ebing and Moll stressed that the fulfilment of sexual desire was significant for individual well-being, partnership and social bonds. In the descriptions of sexual activities, as they appeared in their case studies, the prevalent reproductive norm was pushed into the background. Such an approach was rather new. Already before Freud, Krafft-Ebing and Moll questioned the biological–functionalist approach to sexuality that had its roots in age-old teleological (Aristotelian) as well as modern evolutionary (Darwinian) thinking. As far as sexual behaviour had an aim at all, it was physical pleasure as well as mental satisfaction. It was also seen to contribute to the forging of relationships. Such a viewpoint foreshadowed the modern sexual ethos, the idea that every individual has a right, and perhaps even an obligation to sexual fulfilment, which, together with ideals of partnership, is an essential part of what we view as personal happiness. Krafft-Ebing and Moll also acknowledged that sexual abstinence and dissatisfaction could be harmful to health and well-being. Thus they anticipated the dilemma which Freud elaborated in *Civilization and Its Discontents*: that sexual restraint, considered as an essential precondition for civilization, at the same time may be unhealthy repression and lead to nervous and mental distress (Freud 1930).

The classification of perversions and their relation to 'normal' sexuality

The second feature of sexual modernism concerns how the definition and classification of perversions undermined the differentiation between the normal and the abnormal. Several taxonomies of sexual deviance were developed in late nineteenth-century psychiatry, but the one devised by Krafft-Ebing and adopted by Moll eventually set the tone in medical circles as well as in common sense thinking. Although they paid attention to a wide array of aberrations and deviances, they distinguished four main perversions. The first was contrary sexual feeling, that is various physical and psychological fusions of masculinity and femininity including what we now define as homo- and bisexuality, androgyny, transvestism and trans-sexuality. The second was fetishism, the erotic obsession with certain body-parts, objects or scenarios. The third and fourth were sadism and masochism, terms actually coined by Krafft-Ebing. Some of Krafft-Ebing's neologisms are still current today. These include not only sadism and masochism, but also paedophilia. The terms homosexuality and heterosexuality, which had been introduced in 1869, but were not frequently used during the late nineteenth century, were reintroduced by both Krafft-Ebing and Moll around 1890.

A striking feature of their extensive discussion of these perversions was a shift away from their classification within clear boundaries to an understanding of 'normal' sexuality in the context of deviance and vice versa. They foreshadowed the Freudian notion that the 'libido' consisted of 'component drives' and that a fixed sexual orientation was shaped in developmental stages through specific, either regular or irregular, conversions of various impulses. Krafft-Ebing explained, for example, that sadism and masochism were inherent in normal male and female sexuality, the former being of an active and aggressive and the latter of a passive and submissive nature. Fetishism was also part and parcel of normal sexuality, Krafft-Ebing and Moll argued, because individual taste in sexual attraction and, connected to that, monogamous love were grounded in a distinct preference for particular physical and mental characteristics of one's partner. In addition, their extensive discussion of several forms of gender inversion highlighted the gradual and chance character of the differentiation of the sexes and sexual orientations, and the presumed concomitant bipolar sexual orientations. Exclusive masculinity and femininity and the commonly associated exclusive heterosexual orientations appeared to be mere abstract generalizations. In this way, their approach began to vacillate between the labelling of perversion as pathology and the recognition of the great diversity of desires.

Another striking feature of their work was the highlighting of hetero- and homosexuality as the basic sexual categories. This was closely connected to their shift in perspective from the traditional distinction between procreative and non-procreative acts to the relational dimension of sexuality. Krafft-Ebing's use of the term heterosexual, meaning sexual attraction between a male and a female free from a reproductive goal – and as such initially considered as a perversion – prepared the ground for viewing hetero- and homosexuality as equivalents and identifying other perversions as derived sub-variations of this more fundamental division. This view was shared by Moll. In this way they anticipated a feature of modern sexuality; in the modern sexual configuration it is the gender of one's sexual partner – the other (hetero), the same (homo) or both (bi) – that predominates rather than more specific preferences for other characteristics of one's sexual partner or for certain objects, activities and scenarios. The late nineteenth century French psychologist Alfred Binet, for example, considered fetishism as the fundamental perversion that included all the aberrations by which sexual desire had fixed itself on the 'wrong', that is non-reproductive, goal. If such a fetishist framework for understanding sexual diversity were to have set the tone, our perception and experience of sexuality would be different from what it is nowadays.

The psychological understanding of sexuality

Another crucial feature of sexual modernization was the eclipse of the dominant naturalist approach by a more psychological one. Before the late nineteenth century, the usage of the term sexual predominantly concerned the typical characteristics of the body and the behaviour of males and females. Only in the second half of the nineteenth century did the term begin to be used to indicate a more intricate complex of physical features, behaviours, desires and passions. This new meaning was advanced by the shift in psychiatry in the late nineteenth century from a biomedical perspective that stressed underlying physical processes to one that viewed perversions as functional disorders of an instinct that could not be reduced to the body. Increasing attention focused on the mental aspects of what was now called sexuality.

Although both Krafft-Ebing and Moll speculated about the location of the sexual drive in the nervous system and brain and situated the underlying causes of perversion in heredity and degeneration, such speculations were of little relevance for their interaction with clients. The biomedical perspective receded into the background, and this was largely as a consequence of the prominent position they gave to case histories and the voices of their clients. It was not so much the body or behaviour as such that were crucial in the diagnosis of perversion, but the personal history, thoughts, feelings, perception, desires, imagination, fantasies and dreams of their clients. Sexual desire was increasingly located in a psychological disposition that was at least partly shaped by the social and cultural environment, by sensorial and mental stimuli, memories, storytelling, habits and cultural trends. It was particularly Moll who would in this way foreshadow Freud's understanding of sexuality, which is conceived not as a natural given, but as something that is shaped by mental processes that mediate erratic biological drives, and the possibilities of the body, on the one hand, and cultural prerequisites on the other. This way of thinking advanced the idea that sexual desires are based on a memory trace in the form of mental images of past experiences of satisfaction, which give rise to phantasy and are mediated by signs and language. It is the mental processes that lie behind outward appearance and behaviour that are vital for the determination of sexual orientation, and these processes are partly, in Krafft-Ebing's and Moll's own words, 'unconscious' or 'latent'. An epistemology of depth became the way to make sense of sexuality: the visible surface of the body and behaviour were viewed as signs of something deeply hidden and more essential, the individual subject's interior or 'true self'. Sexual expressions, whether physical, mental or linguistic, were to be subjected to endless psychological interpretation – of which Freud's theory is, of course, the outstanding example.

In Krafft-Ebing's and Moll's work, sexuality thus emerged as a complex of reflexes, bodily sensations, behaviours, experiences and mental processes in which the physical and psychological dimensions interacted with each other. As such, sexuality has indeed become a meaningful and sensitive experience for modern men and women, entailing an array of emotional problems, such as anxious self-scrutiny, fears of being abnormal, worries about sexual attractiveness and achievement, and conflicts between both personal desires and social roles, and fantasies and mundane realities. Krafft-Ebing's and Moll's autobiographical case histories demonstrated that sexuality had become the subject of ceaseless and detailed self-analysis. On the one hand, self-reflection had a redeeming effect since it enabled self-awareness, self-expression and, later, sexual emancipation. On the other, endless brooding more often than not implied uncertainty, uneasiness, inner struggle and frustration.

The close connection between sexuality and personal identity

Closely related to the psychological dimension of sexuality is its strong link to personal identity. Late nineteenth-century psychiatry shifted the focus from a notion of sexual deviance as a passing divergence from the norm to a notion of it as a continuous and essential feature of one's inner being. The psychiatric discourse and the case history method in particular, reflected as well as shaped the experience of sexuality as the quintessence of the individual self. Krafft-Ebing's and Moll's perspective offered a public forum to individuals concerned with articulating their sexual desires and experiences in the form of a personal, autobiographical narrative. Many of them appealed to ideals of authenticity and sincerity to comprehend and justify themselves, and to give coherence to their troubled selves. The form as well as the contents of the psychiatric case history and the sexual autobiography overlapped. Both are patterned and selective narrative reconstructions of past life of the individual from the perspective of the (often troubled) present. Both facilitate the belief that sexual desire and behaviour express something deep and fixed from within the inner self. This presupposition is of course not real in an ontological sense, but is just a way to make sense of sexuality. It has become part of our common sense perception and, as such, it is still a widespread cultural reality in the Western world. Although scholars working in the wake of Michel Foucault's path-breaking work on the history of sexuality have repeatedly criticized the notion that sexual identity is fixed in the self and have emphasized that it is instead a social-historical fabrication, in our society it is very much experienced as though it were an essence that is already there, waiting to be discovered, explored, understood, expressed, liberated and emancipated. Sexologists, psychotherapists, self-help guides, emancipation movements, the mass media and popular psychobabble have only intensified the preoccupation with sexuality as a focal point of the authentic self, personal awareness and self-actualization.

As narrative scripts on which individuals could model their life history, Krafft-Ebing's and Moll's case histories also linked individual introspection and social identification. Their cases reflected and also promoted the emergence of a new experience of sexuality that was closely bound up with the appearance of new kinds of individuals and their grouping into sub-cultural communities, about which several of their clients, especially homosexuals, gave testimony. They not only voiced the comfort of togetherness, but some of them also expressed a critical awareness of the social suppression of their sexuality, and thus the seeds of emancipation were sown.

From the procreative norm to the pleasure and relational dimension of sexuality

The move in psychiatry from a forensic and biomedical focus to sexual psychology entailed that sexuality was increasingly detached from reproduction and that the satisfaction of desire came to the fore. From this it was only a small step to the Freudian conceptualization of the 'libido' and 'pleasure principle', in which desire's only built-in aim is its own satisfaction. In Krafft-Ebing's and Moll's work, in their case histories in particular, the sexual impulse already began to appear as a pleasure wish that yearned neither for reproduction nor for intercourse per se, but only for fulfilment, that is the release of tension through orgasm. This is in line with the steam engine or pressure-cooker model of the sexual drive.

However, Krafft-Ebing and Moll did not conceive of sexuality merely in terms of the pursuit of physical pleasure. Just like Freud, they did not follow the potentially radical consequences of these insights any further. Instead, they suggested a new aim of sexuality by replacing negative evaluations of non-procreative sexuality for a positive evaluation of its relational dimension. The affective longing for physical and psychological union with a partner, the ideal of romantic love, appeared as a purpose in itself. Both love without sex and sexual pleasure without affection, tenderness and attachment were considered to be incomplete. By stressing that the fulfilment of sexual desire played an important binding role for loving relationships, Krafft-Ebing and Moll seemed to tame the dangerous potential of the sexual drive. They anticipated the increasing sexualization of love and marriage in the twentieth century as well as a more accepting attitude towards homosexuality insofar as it was adapted to the relational norm – an attitude which has in recent years taken shape of the legalization of gay marriage all over the Western world.

It was precisely Krafft-Ebing's appreciation of the relational potential of sexuality that contributed to his changed view of homosexuality as an equivalent of heterosexuality rather than as a pathology – a view which Moll then largely adopted. Many homosexuals who expressed themselves in their case histories made clear that partnership was as important to them as sexual gratification. Moll stressed that the manner in which they experienced sexual passions and also love was in no way different from the experiences of heterosexuals in this regard. The prominent position they gave to hetero- and homosexuality as the fundamental sexual categories underlined the shift from a biological–functionalist conception of the sexual impulse as a reproductive instinct towards a view that emphasized erotic desire and pleasure in the context of affection, relationships and personal fulfilment. In this respect, homosexuality appeared to be fundamentally different from other perversions, such as fetishism, masochism, sadism and paedophilia. In contrast to homosexuality, it was difficult to gear these perversions to relational values such as intimacy, privacy, equality, reciprocity and psychological rapprochement. These values also imply that sexuality was burdened with all the psychological complexities of love relationships and the other way around. The marriage between lust and love, involving very different and sometimes contradictory needs and emotions, is not always a stable and happy one.

The social context of the modernization of sexuality

The modern sexual configuration replaced some basic traditional patterns of sexuality. In traditional, collectively and hierarchically organized society, sexuality was largely embedded in a fixed moral order. As a function of social and moral behaviour, it had no distinct existence, but was rather instrumentally embedded in marriage, kinship, fixed gender roles, social status and economic concerns. Sexual morality was dominated by a reproductive imperative; the crucial differentiation was between legitimate procreative sex within marriage and immoral acts that interfered with it, such as adultery, sodomy or masturbation. Moreover, since in traditional societies most people were not individuals in the modern sense, personal sentiment and attraction were subordinated to the calculus of economic security and familial and social interests in choosing a partner.

The psychiatric understanding of perversion, as articulated by Krafft-Ebing, Moll and also Freud, indicated that in the modern Western world sexuality dissociated itself from its near total dependence on, and adaptation to, other social requirements. It began to generate its own meanings as a distinct impulse with its particular psychological mechanisms, which became associated with profound and complex human emotions and anxieties. Framing the experience of sexuality as psychologically significant entails that it was also individualized and internalized; people were made to believe that the game was not so much in the outside world, in human relations and socio-cultural patterns, but foremost in the inner self. Such developments come not only from psychiatric (or psychoanalytic) thinking itself. First, the modernist – that is the overwhelmingly psychological – interpretation relied to a large extent on the self-observations of laypersons who interacted with psychiatry and who were able and often very willing to share their sexual life-stories with medical and psychological experts such as Krafft-Ebing, Moll and Freud. Both parties were agents of culture at large, or at least bourgeois culture; to this day, the dominant Western perspective of sexuality is largely determined by middle-class values. Second, the modern experience of sexuality was rooted in more general and longer-term social and cultural developments, such as the rise of the nuclear family and romantic love; individualization, psychological self-understanding and autobiographical self-analysis in bourgeois circles; social democratization, social and geographical mobility, urbanization, growing affluence and the promotion of, and quest for, enjoyment in consumer capitalism. Such social and cultural trends advanced the emergence of sexuality as a separate and largely internalized sphere in human life. Only at that point was it feasible to define it as a distinct impulse located in the inner self, and to explore its operation in psychological terms. And only at that point did it become possible to liberate and emancipate sexuality, as the precious core of the self, from what people had increasingly begun to experience as its social suppression.

Note

1 This chapter is an abbreviated version of an article published in *Medical History* (Oosterhuis 2012). See also Oosterhuis (2000) and the 2012 special issue of *Medical History* (56:2) devoted to Albert Moll, notably the articles by Sauerteig and Sigusch.

References

Freud, S. (1905). *Three Essays on the Theory of Sexuality*. J. Strachey (ed.), *Standard Edition* 7. London: Hogarth.
Freud, S. (1930). *Civilizations and Its Discontents*, SE 21.
Krafft-Ebing, R. von (1877). Ueber gewisse Anomalien des Geschlechtstriebs und die klinisch-forensische Verwerthung derselben als eines wahrscheinlich functionellen Degenerationszeichens des centralen Nervensystems. *Archiv für Psychiatrie und Nervenkrankheiten* 7, 291–312.
Krafft-Ebing, R. von (1886). *Psychopathia sexualis: Eine klinisch-forensische Studie*. Stuttgart: Ferdinand Enke.
Krafft-Ebing, R. von (1887). *Psychopathia sexualis: Mit besonderer Berücksichtigung der conträren Sexualempfindung: Eine klinisch-forensische Studie*. Stuttgart: Ferdinand Enke (1887–1903, 11 editions).
Krafft-Ebing, R. von (1890). *Neue Forschungen auf dem Gebiet der Psychopathia sexualis: Eine medicinisch-psychologische Studie*. Stuttgart: Ferdinand Enke (1890, 1891, 2 editions).
Krafft-Ebing, R. von (1901a). Neue Studien auf dem Gebiete der Homosexualität. *Jahrbuch für sexuelle Zwischenstufen* 3, 1–36.
Krafft-Ebing, R. von (1901b). Ueber sexuelle Perversionen. In E. von Leyden & F. Klemperer (eds.), *Die deutsche Klinik am Eingang des 20: Jahrhunderts in akademischen Vorlesungen*, Vol. 6. Berlin and Vienna: Urban und Schwarzenberg, 113–154.
Moll, A. (1891). *Die Conträre Sexualempfindung: Mit Benutzung amtlichen Materials*. Berlin: Fischer's Medicinische Buchhandlung/H. Kornfeld (1891, 1893, 1899, 3 editions).
Moll, A. (1897–1898). *Untersuchungen über die Libido sexualis*. Berlin: Fischer's Medicinische Buchhandlung/H. Kornfeld.
Moll, A. (1908). *Das Sexualleben des Kindes*. Leipzig: Verlag von F.C.W. Vogel (1908, 1909, 2 editions).
Moll, A. (1912). *Handbuch der Sexualwissenschaften: Mit besonderer Berücksichtigung der kulturgeschichtlichen Beziehungen*. Leipzig: Verlag von F.C.W. Vogel (1912, 1921, 1926, 3 editions).
Oosterhuis, H. (2000). *Stepchildren of Nature: Krafft-Ebing, Psychiatry, and the Making of Sexual Identity*. Chicago, IL and London: University of Chicago Press.

Oosterhuis, H. (2012). Sexual Modernity in the Works of Richard von Krafft-Ebing and Albert Moll. *Medical History* 56:2, 133–155.

Sauerteig, L. (2012). Loss of Innocence: Albert Moll, Sigmund Freud and the Invention of Childhood Sexuality around 1900. *Medical History* 56:2, 156–183.

Sigusch, V. (2012). The Sexologist Albert Moll – between Sigmund Freud and Magnus Hirschfeld. *Medical History* 56:2, 184–200.

4

THE MYSTERY OF THE ERASED SENTENCE IN FREUD'S *THREE ESSAYS ON THE THEORY OF SEXUALITY*

Patrick Vandermeersch

In the 1915 edition of the *Three Essays*, a sentence has been removed. It has been replaced by a new passage with which we have since become acquainted. The new passage reads as follows:

> By an "instinct" is provisionally to be understood the psychical representative of an endosomatic, continuously flowing source of stimulation, as contrasted with a "stimulus", which is set up by *single* excitations coming from *without*. The concept of instinct is thus one of those lying on the frontier between the mental and the physical. The simplest and likeliest assumption as to the nature of instincts would seem to be that in itself an instinct is without quality, and, as far as mental life is concerned, is only to be regarded as a measure of demand made upon the mind for work. What distinguishes the instincts from one another and endows them with specific qualities is their relation to their somatic sources and to their aims. The source of an instinct is a process of excitation occurring in an organ and the immediate aim of the instinct lies in the removal of this organic stimulus.
>
> *(Freud 1905: 168)*

While the idea of a frontier between the mental and the physical may be reassuring, it is also puzzling. It has given rise to a variety of conjectures, which have largely failed to take into account the erased sentence that the new one has replaced. Let us therefore go back to the 1905 version of the *Three Essays*. The following sentences are the remarks that conclude the discussion of the various perversions in their connection to the erogenic zones:

> If we put together what we have learned from our investigations of positive and negative perversions, it seems plausible to trace them back to a number

of "component instincts", which, however, are not of a primary nature, but are susceptible to further analysis.

(1905: 167–168)

From here on the original text is as follows:

> We can distinguish in them [the component instincts] (in addition to an "instinct" which is not itself sexual and which has its source in motor impulses) a contribution from an organ capable of receiving stimuli (e.g. the skin, the mucous membrane or a sense organ). An organ of this kind will be described in this context as an "erotogenic zone".
>
> *(1905: 168, note 1)*

The key point in the erased sentence is the claim that there is first a basic life instinct that is not sexual per se and that the sexual quality of the libido is acquired only by linking this fundamental drive with parts of the body. At first glance, this does not seem to be such an important element in Freud's theory. Yet closer inspection reveals that it is, in fact, significant. To grasp its importance, it is necessary to study the collaboration between Freud and Jung, which helps us to understand why this sentence had to disappear in order to preserve Freud's own conceptions of the libido theory in the face of the Jungian view (Vandermeersch 1991).

The point of departure of the collaboration between Freud and Jung

Jung was a promising young physician at the Burghölzli hospital near Zurich, an assistant of the famous professor Eugen Bleuler, when he first wrote to Sigmund Freud in 1906. Freud was charmed by Jung's personality and pleased by the fact that he was gaining academic recognition from Zurich. The two men were soon to become friends. At first their collaboration focused on the question of free association, which Freud had developed in his cure of neuroses. Could the same technique be used in order to unveil the meaning behind the seemingly absurd utterances of psychotic patients? Freud would very soon abandon this question of interpretation by means of free association in order to bring the nodal pathological fact of psychotics to the fore. According to him, those patients withdraw the emotional charge from some crucial representations in order to neutralize them. In conformity with Freud's own model of the psychic apparatus, these representations become "projected", i.e. treated as representations stemming from outside the subject. Therefore, they are considered as "true", like the other objects of perception of the external world. Thus the withdrawal of the libido was the core of the psychotic process. Projection followed as a consequence of it and was in fact nothing special. It was *not* a defence mechanism but a normal, automatic procedure of our psychic functioning. A few lines later a new, important element comes in as Freud unexpectedly equates "emotion" with "libido". Withdrawal of the emotional charge is called "withdrawal of the libido", and Freud does not give any explanation for why this is so (Freud–Jung 1974: letter 22–25).

For Jung and Bleuler, the idea of conceiving the withdrawal of the emotional charge as the core of the outbreak of a psychosis was not at all a strange one. They had written a lot on "affectivity", which they thought consolidated the psyche as a unity. What Freud had written seemed to be in line with their views. But can this be the case with regard to his equation of affectivity and libido? Bleuler and Jung knew how much psychotic patients displayed autoeroticism. They masturbated without any shame and liked to play with their excrements – indeed, psychiatric clinics in those days usually had tiled walls so that they could be cleaned easily. So, we meet here from the beginning the central issue of the Freud–Jung debate: How can you develop a theory that links affectivity and libido?

What is autoerotism?

For Freud, a regression to autoerotism is the core of the psychotic process. Is there, however, some sort of purpose to this regression? Jung is convinced of just such a purpose. He mentions a patient saying, "Everything that happens has something so *gripping* about it" (Freud–Jung: letter 72J). Autoerotism seems to provide shelter and a sense of security. Freud does not provide a counter-argument to this claim at this point.

Jung develops his position by adding another idea. Autoerotism is not just a mechanical interplay of parts of the body. If autoerotism offers security, this is because it reminds us of an earlier stage where the rudiments of psychic functioning were still active. And these rudiments refer not only to our personal past, but also to a phylogenetic heritage, the vestiges of the evolution of mankind which are present in our archaic body/mind unity. Our mind contains not only a personal unconscious, stemming from our personal histories, but also a more primitive one, which we share with other humans. This collective unconscious stems from our common, evolutionary history. Just as our body contains and still uses parts of its earlier functioning, so too we can find remainders of primitive functioning in our mind.

At this point, the parallel between psychotic delusions and religious mythology can be drawn. Jung knew the Schreber case, and he gave Freud Schreber's famous autobiography in which the President of the Court of Dresden claims he was elected to become God's wife. Schreber developed a complicated personal theology, which featured plenty of erotic symbolism that was not so different from the gnostic systems we are familiar with today. According to Jung, the regression to autoerotism is not just a discharge of libidinal energy in a mechanical way as Freud had conceived it. It is a regression to a previous stage of psychical functioning where some old elements of the phylogenesis persisted. There were also archaic forms of thinking that belonged to this phylogenetic heritage, which can be found in mythology and religion and are the precursors of rational thinking. It is for this reason that the delusions of psychotics look so much like mythology. It also explains why the religious delusions of Schreber warranted investigation.

Homosexuality enters the debate

Homosexuality is a new element that is added to the ongoing debate. Freud notes that in many forms of psychosis (in fact he uses the then more general, but nowadays disputable, term of "paranoia"), there is undoubtedly homosexuality at stake. Thus he concludes that in those cases there is not a withdrawal of the whole of autoerotism, but only of a part of it, the homosexual part. While scrutinizing this problem within the framework of psychosis, Freud becomes aware of the more universal presence of homosexual elements in the human mind, his own in particular. It is noteworthy that the article on Schreber was written by Freud while he holidayed in Sicily with Sandor Ferenczi as his travel companion, and that the latter did not hide his homosexual feelings for Freud (Simmons 2006).

Thus it is by dealing with the more general presence of homosexual elements in the human mind in general, and his own in particular, that Freud goes back to the function of homosexuality in what he still calls "paranoia". He does not seem to notice that he thereby overlooks the difference between the function of homosexuality in both cases. Further on, Freud's Schreber analysis focuses on the question of how the homosexual part of the libido is caught in the process of de-cathexis. But in this respect, another point is missed. Jung's question about the relation between psychotic regression and the reappearance of primitive religious fantasy is neglected, despite the fact that Schreber stated explicitly that he wrote his memoirs for the benefit of the psychology of religion (Freud 1905: 140, 1911a: 10).

At first glance, it does not seem difficult to shed light on the core homosexual elements in Schreber's delusions. Nevertheless, they are different throughout the course of his illness (if one should not indeed speak of his *illnesses*). In his first delusions, pertaining to the time of his first stay in the psychiatric clinic of Flechsig, he is terrified by the idea of being sexually assaulted by the medical personnel there. Later, during the lengthy period in which he is committed to an asylum, Schreber becomes convinced that he will be transformed into a woman in order to become God's wife and give birth to a new race once the old world and its inhabitants have gone.

If we place Schreber's "homosexuality" under greater scrutiny, we can distinguish two different elements. First, there is the theme of anal penetration, easily recognizable in his delusional experiences that the divine spirit pushes his bowels back and forth and in the fact that the lavatories are always occupied so as to prevent him from defecating. Freud describes this part of Schreber's delusional experience at length, but it plays no part in his psychoanalytic elucidation. Second, there is the theme of wanting to become a woman, prominently exhibited by Schreber. Yet is this transsexual wish identical with homosexuality? It is worth noting in this regard that this wish to become a woman is in no way related to castration, as one might expect after Freud's case study of Little Hans. Of course, it might be that the fear of and/or wish for castration has been hidden by repression, but this is not a topic in Freud's analysis. According to Schreber's delusional experience, every nerve in his body will, through their contact with

God's nerves, be gradually transformed into that of a female until he has become part of a fusional unity with the deity.

All this becomes more puzzling when we consider the theory Freud develops in the third, theoretical, part of his essay. Freud sketches the following picture. A baby is originally a mosaic of erotogenic zones, which give pleasure without giving the body the sense of being a unity or organized whole. This is followed by the stage of narcissism, in which an image of oneself develops. One loves this image, wherein a predominant value is also given to one's own genitals. From this point on, once one has become an individual (or, as we would say today, one is no longer part of the maternal body), we fall in love with other individuals of the same sex and admire their bodies: they are just as we would like to be. From the basis of these narcissistic and homosexual stages, one usually proceeds to heterosexuality. Why? Freud does not provide a justification, though perhaps we could supplement what he has said as follows: in our admiration for strong men (Freud only speaks about men in this text) and in our realization that they love to have sex with women, we start to do the same, driven by mimicry.

It is nevertheless difficult to fit the Schreber case into that framework, and, in fact, Freud does not try to locate Schreber's psychosexual development within the scheme just described. The massive presence of anal pleasure and the wish to become a woman are both dismissed by Freud in this third, theoretical part of his essay. One cannot but think that these themes were just the preliminaries, the foreplay, before dealing with the more general theme of homosexuality, which he could now discuss without paying further heed to the preliminary themes.

But Freud could not escape the question of why Schreber became psychotic. Indeed, he tries to deal with it, though in doing so renders his own theoretical account even more questionable. He goes back to his first intuition, which was that the nucleus of psychosis consists in de-cathexis, the withdrawal of the libido from external reality, and that projection is only a consequence of this, given the structure of the psychic apparatus. Freud is happy to discover in the experience of the "end of the world", as described by Schreber, the expression of this de-cathexis. Freud then asks whether the de-cathexis of the libido is sufficient to explain this inner catastrophe of the "end of the world", this break between the subject and the external reality. It might be expected that Freud would delve deeper into the fact, mentioned by him, that only a part of the libido, i.e. the homosexual part, has been withdrawn. But that is not the issue he draws attention to. Instead, he suddenly introduces the opposition between two drives, the ego-drives (plural) and the sexual drive (singular), and he asks why the ego-drives are not sufficient to sustain the relation with external reality. It is in this context that he writes the following sentences, which will become the point of departure for Jung's attempt to broaden the scope of the libido theory:

> Are we to suppose that a general detachment of the libido from the external world would be an effective enough agent to account for the "end of the world"? Or would not the ego-cathexes which still remained in existence

have been sufficient to maintain *rapport* with the external world? To meet this difficulty we should either have to assume that what we call libidinal cathexis (that is, interest emanating from erotic sources) coincides with interest in general, or we should have to consider the possibility that a very widespread disturbance in the distribution of the libido may bring about a corresponding disturbance in the ego-cathexes. But these are problems which we are still quite helpless and incompetent to solve. It would be otherwise if we could start off from some well-grounded theory of instincts; but in fact we have nothing of the kind at our disposal. We regard instinct as being the concept on the frontier-line between the somatic and the mental, and see in it the psychical representative of organic forces. Further, we accept the popular distinction between ego-instincts and a sexual instinct . . . We can no more dismiss the possibility that disturbances of the libido may react upon the ego-cathexes than we can overlook the converse possibility – namely, that a secondary or induced disturbance of the libidinal processes may result from abnormal changes in the ego.

(Freud 1911a: 73–75)

But how should we understand the "ego" in the wake of Freud's introduction of a narcissistic and a homosexual stage in human development? This should have been the central issue of his own reading of Schreber. What about the special religious quality of Schreber's delirium? This illustrates that religion is not just the anchor for repression and morality, but that there are other, very seducing, aspects in religious phantasms. Freud does not answer these questions, whereas Jung tries to do so. And one must acknowledge that in attempting to answer these questions, he could see himself as being on the right Freudian track.

Jung's phylogenetic view on the libido

Jung would come to regret the fact that he had left the analysis of Schreber's autobiography to Freud. While Freud was writing this analysis, Jung himself started an article of his own on the writings of another psychotic patient, Miss Miller. The first part of Jung's book, entitled *Wandlungen und Symbole der Libido (Transformations and Symbolisms of the Libido)*, was published in 1911 in the same issue of the *Jahrbuch für psychoanalytische und psychopathologische Forschungen* as Freud's Schreber. Already in the opening sentences, Jung states that his aim is to interpret individual psychological productions in the light of phylogenesis, i.e. the biological and psychical evolution of mankind. There is little shocking to be found in this first part of the essay wherein he describes parallels between individual and mythological fantasy systems.

The second part, however, published a year later (Jung 1912), opens with a large theoretical section on the libido theory. It starts with the sentences from Freud's article on Schreber that were quoted above. How, as happens in Schreber's psychosis, does the sexual drive strike back at the ego-drives? For Jung this is really the crux of the issue, and Freud is at least honest enough to state it so openly.

Jung thought that there could be an answer to this problem, and crucially it is one that has already been suggested in the definition of the libido Freud provides in the *Three Essays*. Jung continues by quoting the sentence that, as we have seen, Freud erased from later editions of the text.

The theory Jung develops can be sketched as follows. Originally, there is only one drive, in which auto-conservation and propagation cannot be distinguished. In unicellular beings, growth and multiplication are one and the same process. Little by little, the function of propagation becomes a separate process. It becomes more complicated, leading to a point where two sexes should be united, where they should learn to build a nest and so forth. These later developments require the rudiments of thinking. Thinking requires that one stops acting in an entirely conditioned way, and therefore one needs fantasy, i.e. the introduction of a delay between receiving information from the senses and acting. Propagation is the first realm where this happens, and the sexual content of mythology is the result of this. It is for this reason that the content of mythology is so sexual.

In the course of this process, the two functions of sexuality (as the individual's care for him/herself and for his/her offspring) grow apart. When it comes to human beings, rational thinking is no longer a sexual fantasy, and one can even see how "ego-drives" can oppose the "sexual drive". Repression, as described by Freud, is in operation at that level. From a phylogenetic point of view, this presupposes that the broad primal sexuality has been differentiated into ego-instincts, on the one hand, and the more specific sexuality, the "recent sexuality" as Jung calls it in his text, on the other. It is now possible to understand why, in the case of a deep regression, as in psychosis, one falls back to the more primitive layers of our psyche, the strata of mythological thinking. It is for this reason that psychotic delusions and mythological systems are so much alike.

Obviously, it was Jung's functionalist grounding of mythology in the evolutionary process that Freud found deeply problematic. If Jung were right, religion could claim to be a necessary stage in the development of mankind. What is more, a regression back to that stage could be understandable and even helpful as a kind of rejuvenation, as Jung would put it in the further development of his theory. Freud seems to have foreseen that Jung would introduce this view; as soon as he had read the first draft of Jung's *Wandlungen*, he started to write the "Formulations on the Two Principles of Mental Functioning", which he explicitly intended as a companion piece to the Schreber article (Freud 1911b). In this text, he underscores the point that erotic phantasies do not stem from the early stages of childhood in the same way as the fantasizing function in general. They emerge later, once the use of fantasy has become a function. Religious fantasy is not the mother of rational thinking.

Conclusion: Freud's distress – homosexuality and religion

Did Schreber's autobiography enable Freud to attain some new insights? It seems to me that it did not. It did not even lead to new well-formulated questions.

Freud focused on what he called the "paternal complex", and he carried out his analysis in the same way he would have done in cases of neurosis. It is worthwhile indicating that the recently introduced Oedipus complex does not play a part in his analysis. Schreber's mother is completely absent. If we turn to the new questions he raised concerning psychosis, religion and homosexuality, it is noteworthy that they all remained without answer and became even more confused.

As far as schizophrenia is concerned (the term can now be used because Bleuler coined it in a book published the same year as Freud's Schreber study (Freud 1911a) and Freud was aware of the pending shift in terminology), Freud points in a rather small part of the text to the de-cathexis of external reality as experienced by Schreber in his end-of-the-world delusion. This leads him to the problem of projection that remains unsolved – he announces a special text on it, but it will never appear.

Although in the foreword to his book Schreber claims it may have value for the understanding of religion, and although Freud quotes this claim, he says nothing about religion in his article. Furthermore, in the associated article on the two principles of mental functioning, he deals with religion only in its function of supporting morality, which bears no relation to the form taken by Schreber's religious experience.

It is also necessary to ask about homosexuality. Here we meet the paradox that the theoretical model introducing a homosexual stage between autoeroticism and heterosexual love does not at all encompass the use of homosexuality in the case study, where homosexuality is conceived as transsexuality. Schreber wants to become a woman and to do so, it should be insisted, without wrestling with castration fantasies and thus not according to what will become the classical Oedipal scheme.

Putting all this together, we come to another puzzling conclusion: given that Freud has become convinced that the core of the paranoia process consists of the withdrawal of a part of the libidinal cathexis, namely the homosexual part, Schreber's case would imply that there is a link between homosexuality and religion, insofar as weight is given to the religious content of his delusion.

The perplexity of Freud's position appears in the erasure of the sentence. And the new sentences replacing it, especially "the source of an instinct is a process of excitation occurring in an organ and the immediate aim of the instinct lies in the removal of this organic stimulus", see Freud escape from what he met at "the frontier between the mental and the physical" into a pure mechanistic theory.

References

Freud, S. (1905). *Three Essays on the Theory of Sexuality*. J. Strachey (ed.), *Standard Edition 7*. London: Hogarth.

Freud, S. (1911a). Psycho-Analytic Notes on an Autobiographical Account of a Case of Paranoia (Dementia paranoides), *SE 12*.

Freud, S. (1911b). Formulations on the Two Principles of Mental Functioning, *SE 12*.

Freud–Jung (1974). *The Freud-Jung Letters*. London: The Hogarth Press and Routledge & Kegan Paul.

Jung, C.G. (1912). *Psychology of the Unconscious: A Study of the Transformations and Symbolisms of the Libido*. Transl. B.M. Hinkle, Princeton, NJ: Princeton University Press, 2001.

Simmons, L. (2006). *Freud's Italian Journey*. Amsterdam: Rodopi.

Vandermeersch, P. (1991). *Unresolved Questions in the Freud/Jung Debate: On Psychosis, Sexual Identity and Religion*. Leuven: Leuven University Press.

5
FREUD READS KRAFFT-EBING
The case of sadism and masochism

Jens De Vleminck

Introduction

In the current Diagnostic and Statistical Manual of Mental Disorders, *DSM-5*, the once illustrious and imaginative psychiatric taxa of sadism and masochism are buried under an overwhelming proliferation of disorders. Both taxa are part of a group of "paraphilic disorders based on *anomalous activity preferences*", further specified as "the *algolagnic disorders*, which involve pain and suffering (sexual masochism disorder and sexual sadism disorder)" (American Psychiatric Association 2013: 685, 694–697). Nevertheless, that both 'sadism' ('sadistic') and 'masochism' ('masochistic') are familiar concepts which are part of our everyday language is no doubt due to the popularization and the common use of psychoanalytic jargon. Despite his structural contribution to the widespread use of the terminology, Freud did not coin the terms 'sadism' and 'masochism' himself, neither did he embed these concepts in the disciplines of psychiatry and sexology. It was the French lexicographer Pierre Boiste (1765–1824) who honoured the French novelist D.A.F. de Sade (1740–1814) by coining the eponym 'sadism'. The latter was ultimately picked up and immortalized in psychiatry by the German-Austrian psychiatrist Richard von Krafft-Ebing. This happened in the fifth edition (1890) of his *Psychopathia Sexualis*, the former 'bible' of psychiatry and sexology. In that very same edition, Krafft-Ebing himself first coined the concept of 'masochism', after the Austrian historian and novelist Leopold von Sacher-Masoch (1836–1895). In this way, both of Krafft-Ebing's psychiatric concepts would find their way into the developing domain of psychoanalysis. Both sadism and masochism are introduced into psychoanalytic discourse in the first edition of Freud's *Three Essays on the Theory of Sexuality* (1905a). They have remained key concepts for psychoanalytical metapsychology ever since and are omnipresent in the work of Melanie Klein, amongst others.

This chapter aims to develop a brief genealogy of both sadism and masochism. Before the introduction of the death instinct, they served for many years as the only concepts through which Freud dealt with the complex theme of human aggressiveness. From the very beginning, however, both sadism and masochism were problematic concepts for him. We will argue that the very specific way in which Freud takes over the concepts from Krafft-Ebing, re-conceptualizing and anchoring them in psychoanalytic metapsychology, is of crucial importance for understanding Freud's subsequent struggle with them, which continues until his final writings. More specifically, Freud's re-conceptualization of both sadism and masochism in accordance with the model of the hysterical body, including the prevalence of the erotogenic zones, is of determining importance in the *Three Essays*. It is argued that Freud's *modus operandi* is at the origin of both sadism's and masochism's problematic status. We will develop this argument by first taking a look at Krafft-Ebing's *Psychopathia Sexualis*. Subsequently, we make a reconstruction of how both sadism and masochism are given shape in Freud's *Three Essays*. Finally, it will be argued that Freud's research matrix of hysteria functions as the bed of Procrustes for both sadism and masochism. This is because the matrix of hysteria not only makes an adequate understanding of both sadism and masochism impossible but equally impedes a more nuanced interpretation of human aggressiveness in psychoanalytic metapsychology.

Sadism and masochism in the *Psychopathia Sexualis*

Although he is also a reference figure in the history of forensic psychiatry, the German-Austrian psychiatrist Richard von Krafft-Ebing is primarily known as the founding father of sexology. His *Psychopathia Sexualis* is widely accepted to be the foundational work for the scientific study of human sexuality, a field still in its infancy at the end of the nineteenth century. *Psychopathia Sexualis* offers an overview of both sexological physiology and psychology and is of groundbreaking importance for the origin of the modern scientific research domain of sexological pathology as an autonomous discipline (Ellenberger 1970: 297). Krafft-Ebing's 'bible of psychopathology' evolved from a collection of 45 clinical vignettes in its first edition (1886) into an extensive collection of 238 case histories in its final, posthumously published edition (1903). Combining a clinical analysis of these cases and a synthetic overview of the status of perversions in nineteenth-century psychiatry, Krafft-Ebing's encyclopaedia of the perversions was considered the absolute standard in its research domain.

In the preface to the *Psychopathia Sexualis*, Krafft-Ebing refers to the work of the German philosopher Friedrich von Schiller (1759–1805) in order to highlight love and hunger as the two fundamental human instincts (*Triebe*).[1] In accordance with the then prevalent functional conception of the instincts, Krafft-Ebing conceptualizes the sexual instinct in terms of a *Geschlechtstrieb*, i.e., as being *naturally* directed towards procreation. According to this view, functional deviations of the latter norm necessarily imply pathology. Each deviation from the natural reproductive function implies a perversion. In the wake of the prevailing 'degeneration theory', understanding pathology as a sign of constitutional degeneration (Porter 2002), perversions are interpreted by Krafft-Ebing as being "functional signs of degeneration" (*funktionelle Degenerationszeichen*) (Krafft-Ebing 1903: 32). The perverse condition thus necessary presupposed a congenital and hereditarily determined pathological condition of the central nervous system. The perversions, being defined as deviations of the sexual function, were divided by Krafft-Ebing into four categories: the *paradoxia* (sexual excitement occurring independently of the period of physiological processes in the generative organs), the *anaesthesia* (absence of sexual instinct), the *hyperaesthesia* (increased desire, satyriasis) and the *paraesthesia* (perversion of the sexual instinct, i.e. excitability of the sexual functions to inadequate stimuli) (1903: 34). For Krafft-Ebing, however, it is only this latter category, consisting of sadism, masochism, fetishism and 'antipathic sexuality' (*conträre Sexualempfindung*), that should be considered a sexual perversion *stricto sensu* (1903: 34–35). The first two of these four basic or core perversions were introduced in psychiatric discourse by Krafft-Ebing himself, more specifically in the fifth edition (1890) of his *Psychopathia Sexualis*. There, Krafft-Ebing acknowledges sadism and masochism to be "the fundamental forms of psycho-sexual perversions, which may make their appearance at any point of the domain of sexual aberration" (1903: 143). The extreme character of these perversions must be exclusively understood on the basis of their being determined by hereditary degeneration and, as such, can be seen as an argument against the decisive influence of accidental factors (Sulloway 1979: 287–288). Following Krafft-Ebing, we first examine sadism and masochism as they are defined independently, before going into the nature of their interrelatedness.

Sadism

Sadism is defined by Krafft-Ebing as "the association of active cruelty and violence with lust" (Krafft-Ebing 1903: 53). More specifically, it is:

> [t]he experience of sexual pleasurable sensations (including orgasm) produced by acts of cruelty, bodily punishment afflicted on one's own person or when witnessed in others, be they animals or human beings. It may also consist of an innate desire to humiliate, hurt, wound or even destroy others in order thereby to create sexual pleasure in oneself.
>
> *(1903: 53)*

Except for the fact that it always implies a condition of hereditary degeneration, sadism is understood by Krafft-Ebing as synonymous with a wide spectrum of manifestations. This implies, for instance, that cruelty, which is always accompanied by sexual pleasure, can occur both in reality and in phantasy. Krafft-Ebing has a gradual conception of aggressiveness and cruelty, which varies from lust murders to ideal sadism where merely the lust for superiority is emphasized.

The diverse spectrum of expressions has, however, two characteristics in common, and both of these have their origin in hereditary degeneration. First, sadism is the expression of extreme sexual excitement, giving rise to an excessive loss of the self in an object-oriented activity, which has the infliction of pain as its most intense means. Second, sadism also has roots in the excessive manifestation of the natural, active character of the male. The male needs to have the necessary aggressiveness at his disposal in order to conquer the female, who is passive by nature. The active domination of the female by the male can debouch into sadism and can lead to violence and destruction. "If both these constituent elements occur together – the abnormally intensified impulse to a violent reaction towards the object of the stimulus, and the abnormally intensified desire to conquer a woman, – then the most violent outbreaks of sadism occur" (1903: 56). "Sadism", he adds, "is thus nothing else than an excessive and monstrous pathological intensification of phenomena – possible, too, in normal conditions in rudimentary forms – which accompany the psychical sexual life, particularly in males" (1903: 56).

Krafft-Ebing makes a distinction between 'perversions', on the one hand, and so-called 'perversities', which can occur occasionally or can be part of normal sexual life (e.g. kissing leading to biting), on the other (1903: 60). Despite degeneration and excess being characteristics of perversions, a certain continuity is displayed with regard to normality, in which so-called 'atavistic phenomena' (*atavistische Erscheinungen*) can be retraced (1903: 60). In the case of the sadistic conjunction of cruelty and pleasure, Krafft-Ebing refers to a cannibalistic theory in which excessive, sexual aggression is understood according to the model of hunger. Correspondingly, sadism is an atavistic manifestation of the devouring of the partner during the sexual act, as is the case in some invertebrates. As such, sadism implies the supposition of an original coincidence of hunger and sexual appetite (Krafft-Ebing 1903: 163; Sulloway 1979: 291–292; Oosterhuis 2000: 68).

Masochism

Krafft-Ebing concisely defines masochism as "the association of passively endured cruelty and violence with lust" (1903: 86). He elaborates this definition as follows: "Masochism is the opposite of sadism. While the latter is the desire to cause pain and use force, the former is the wish to suffer pain and be subjected to force" (1903: 86). Like sadism, masochism equally seems to refer to a very diverse and gradually differentiated range of phenomena. Nevertheless, masochistic cruelty never goes as far as the most extreme sadistic manifestations, which can result in severe injuries or even death. Contrary to what is the case in masochistic phantasies, in reality masochism is limited by the 'instinct of self-preservation' (*Selbsterhaltungstrieb*) (1903: 96–97). The essence of masochism is the submission to and the humiliation and abuse by a person of the opposite sex, accompanied by sexual pleasure (1903: 87). Krafft-Ebing mentions two specific criteria for perverse masochism, which have to be understood on the basis of masochism's degenerative nature. Just as sadism is the excessive manifestation of the active male nature, Krafft-Ebing's two criteria of masochism are related to the natural characteristics of the passive, female nature. The first and most important determinant of masochism is sexual arousal, which is an excessive state of pleasurable exaltation that originates in whatever sensations come from the sexual object – including abuse. The second root of masochism is related to the phenomenon of dependency on the sexual object. The latter phenomenon is exhibited in an excessive way in the abnormal though not perverse phenomenon of 'sexual bondage' (*geschlechtliche Hörigkeit*) (1903: 149). Although implying gradually different manifestations, this abnormal expression of lustful submission to and dependency towards the person of the opposite sex must be qualitatively distinguished from masochism (1903: 152). The dependency and submission, both excessively displayed in sexual bondage, originate in the fear of losing the object, in the desire to please the object and in the extraordinary degree of love by which the female nature is characterized (1903: 149).

Despite sexual bondage and masochism being two distinct phenomena, Krafft-Ebing holds the former to be an explanatory key that can unlock the meaning of the latter. This is because masochism is characterized by a similar unconditional submission to a dominant object. In the case of sexual bondage, this submission serves merely as a means, whereas for masochism excessive submissiveness must be considered to be an end in itself. Ultimately, for Krafft-Ebing, the qualitative difference between sexual bondage and masochism essentially goes back to the factor of hereditary degeneration. It is this latter factor which, according to Krafft-Ebing, necessitates differentiating masochism from passive flagellation, although the latter can in some cases function as an extreme expression of a masochistic, degenerated nature.[2]

Another related element is the question concerning the role of pain in masochism. Krafft-Ebing is very clear in denying any inextricable link between masochism and pain. He claims that pain cannot be understood as an essential part of masochism. In those cases where pain is effectively part of the lust in submission, it merely serves as a means by which the submission occurs. The pain is subordinate to the pleasure experienced by the masochist in submitting to the volition of the sexual object. Krafft-Ebing holds that in phantasy the masochist ascribes male psychosexual characteristics to the dominant object. The sadistic female partner functions as the masochistic ideal of the latter object. This is the case because, as Krafft-Ebing points out, masochists are mostly men. Those masochistic men assume a female role and as such submit themselves to the will of their mistresses. Krafft-Ebing suggests a link between masochism, on the one hand, and sexual inversion and partial female psychosexuality, on the other. In contrast to sadism, which occurs in both men and women, Krafft-Ebing does only explain masochism by making an appeal to the theory of original bisexuality.[3] In the course of the 1890s, Krafft-Ebing has already appealed to the latter theory in presenting an explanation of inversion (Sulloway 1979: 294–295; Oosterhuis 2000: 66). From the perspective of this theory, masochism could be seen as an expression of a developmental disorder in the subject's mono-sexual evolution. Krafft-Ebing relies on the very same theory when raising the question concerning the mutual interrelation of sadism and masochism. By anchoring the theory of bisexuality in his *Psychopathia Sexualis*, Krafft-Ebing is largely responsible for its further scientific proliferation (Angelides 2001: 36). Around the turn of the century, the constitutional bisexuality of man has more or less become a universally accepted idea.

Sadism and masochism

At the end of his discussion of masochism, Krafft-Ebing explicitly raises the question of how masochism relates to sadism and vice versa. He acknowledges that:

> [t]he perfect counterpart of masochism is sadism. While in the former there is a desire to suffer and be subjected to violence, in the latter the wish is to inflict pain and use of violence. The parallel is perfect. All the acts and situations used by the sadist in the active role become the object of the desire of the masochist in the passive role . . . Thus masochism and sadism represent perfect counterparts. It is also in harmony with this that the individuals affected with these perversions regard the opposite perversion in the other sex as their ideal.
>
> *(1903: 140–141)*

The development of the perversion is not determined by occasional experiences of pain, according to Krafft-Ebing. He argues that:

> [l]ust in the infliction of pain and lust in inflicted pain appear but as two different sides of the same psychical process, of which the primary and essential thing is the consciousness of active and passive subjection, in which the combination of cruelty and lustful pleasure has only a secondary psychological significance. Acts of cruelty serve to express this subjection; first because they are the most extreme means for the expression of this relation; and, again, because they represent the most intense effects that one person, either with or without coitus, can exert on another.
>
> *(1903: 142)*

Krafft-Ebing's attention is particularly drawn towards a very specific type of case, i.e. those cases in which sadism and masochism occur as combined in one and the same individual. At the same time, however, the latter cases put him in an awkward position from a theoretical point of view. For Krafft-Ebing stresses that, in those cases where sadism and masochism occur simultaneously, either the active or the passive submission is at the very heart of the perverse desires. In any case, either one of the perversions is always "markedly predominant", according to Krafft-Ebing (1903: 142). By making an appeal to the imagination, however, the predominant perversion is able to release its opposite. In the end, though, the latter is abandoned in favour of the 'original', predominant perversion. The consideration of a simultaneous sadism and masochism brings Krafft-Ebing to think of inversion and the theory of bisexuality. As a matter of fact, the latter theory originates in the same current of psychiatric thinking that maintained both the cannibalistic theory of intercourse and the idea of 'desiring to be a victim' (1903: 432, note 63). Although he is familiar with the theory of bisexuality, Krafft-Ebing never explicitly takes it into account in order to explain sadism or masochism. Nevertheless, towards the end of his career, he certainly went in the direction of such a theoretical assumption. This is interesting given the fact that it is exactly the assumption of an original and congenital bisexuality that is given a central place by Freud in his *Three Essays on the Theory of Sexuality*. At least in two instances, Freud explicitly makes an appeal to this original bisexuality. Thus, asides from inversion, the paired opposites sadism-masochism are also explained by referring to bisexuality. Although Freud confesses to having first adopted the notion of bisexuality from Wilhelm Fliess (Freud 1905a: 220, note 1), there is no doubt that he is, at the very least, just as indebted to Krafft-Ebing. This must be so given that the latter, being the contemporary authority in Freud's research domain, contributed to the importance and the credibility of the theory of bisexuality.

In what follows, we will illustrate that Freud relies *almost exclusively* on the information from Krafft-Ebing's *Psychopathia Sexualis* for the introduction and conceptualization of sadism and masochism in the *Three Essays*. We will argue that Freud's rethinking of the concept of perversion is related to his analysis of the psychoneuroses. In the latter analysis, hysteria functions as the psychoneurosis *par excellence*, i.e. hysteria is the predominant model in the discussion of the psychoneurotic condition in general. Yet the following question remains: What are the implications of holding hysteria as the prototype of psychoneurosis for the conceptualization of sadism and masochism? Before discussing the specific status of sadism and masochism, we have to question the *general* status of the perversions in Freud.

The concept of perversion in the *Three Essays*

The first edition of the *Three Essays on the Theory of Sexuality* was published two years after the edition of *Psychopathia Sexualis* (1903) that, though posthumously published, was the last to be revised by Krafft-Ebing himself. By devoting the first essay of his 'triptych' to the perversions or 'sexual aberrations', Freud places himself in the tradition of nineteenth-century psychiatry in general and of Krafft-Ebing in particular. Freud's interest in the perversions, however, is not an end in itself, but is related to his research into psychoneurosis and, more specifically, hysteria. Prior to the *Three Essays*, Freud's analysis of hysteria was determined by two factors: congenital bisexuality and the organic repression of the erotogenic zones (Van Haute & Geyskens 2012). In the same year as the *Three Essays*, moreover, Freud published his Dora case as *Fragment of an Analysis of a Case of Hysteria* (Freud 1905b). In what follows, we argue that from the outset Freud's assumptions about the relation between perversions and hysteria – the latter being his model of psychoneuroses – are of determining importance for the conceptualization of sadism and masochism in the *Three Essays*.

By opening his *Three Essays* with a presentation of the perversions, Freud was in fact broaching the central topic of contemporary psychiatry. As such, the first essay can be identified as part of a strategic gesture. For while at first sight the essay seems to conform to the psychiatric tradition of that time, the Freudian discourse immediately dissociates itself from this tradition, developing a different discourse. It should be clear that Freud's critique of what he calls 'popular opinion' in fact implies a critique of the classical psychiatric tradition (with Krafft-Ebing as its main representative) that defends the functionalistic conception of the sexual instinct as a *Geschlechtstrieb* directed towards reproduction (Freud 1905a: 135). For, at that time, there was a "virtually *unargued unanimity*" about understanding the sexual instinct according to the model of hunger, as Schiller had earlier done (Davidson 1987: 260). Freud clearly takes a stand against this position: "We have every reason to believe, however, that these views give a very false picture of the true situation. If we look into them more closely we shall find that they contain a number of errors, inaccuracies and hasty conclusions" (Freud 1905a: 135). Freud challenges the prevailing discourse by using its own presuppositions against it. He discusses the perversions in terms of "deviations" from "what is assumed to be normal", either with respect to "the *sexual object*", "the person from whom sexual attraction proceeds" or with respect to "the *sexual aim*", "the act towards which the instinct tends" (1905a: 135–136). This strategy leads towards a deconstruction of the functionalistic conception of sexuality.

Taking sexual inversion as a starting point, Freud argues that the sexual instinct is not naturally directed towards a specific object. When discussing the "deviations in respect of the sexual aim", including sadism and masochism, Freud in a similar way denounces the presence of an a priori, natural aim:

> The normal sexual aim is regarded as being the union of the genitals in the act known as copulation, which leads to a release of the sexual tension and a temporary extinction of the sexual instinct – a satisfaction analogous to the sating of hunger.
>
> *(1905a: 149)*

Focusing on this norm, Freud defines the perversions as:

> [s]exual activities which either (a) extend, in an anatomical sense, beyond the regions of the body that are designed for sexual union, or (b) linger over the immediate relations to the sexual object which should normally be traversed rapidly on the pad towards the final sexual aim.
>
> *(1905a: 150)*

Freud maintains that "even in the most normal sexual process we may detect rudiments which, if they had developed, would have led to the deviations described as 'perversions'" (1905a: 149). In this context, he prefers drawing on those examples that are of central importance in his analysis of hysteria, such as "touching and looking" and the "high sexual esteem" of the "kiss" (1905a: 149–150).

One could argue that the continuity between perversion and normality that is suggested by Freud is not entirely new. As a representative of the functionalistic tradition, Krafft-Ebing also suggests a link between perversion and normality. Despite this link, there remains for him an important discontinuity based on the decisive criterion of hereditary degeneration in the case of perversion. Unlike Krafft-Ebing, Freud explicitly renounces the idea of conceiving perversions as "indications of degeneration or disease", asserting instead that perversions "are constituents which are rarely absent from the sexual life of healthy people" (1905a: 160). Perversion and normality are understood as "mere variations" between which it is impossible "to draw a sharp line" (1905a: 161). Unlike Krafft-Ebing, Freud stresses a radical continuity between normality and perversion, and he understands normality on the basis of perversion: "No healthy person, it appears, can fail to make some addition that might be called perverse to the normal sexual aim" (1905a: 160). Instead of conceiving perversion as the *privatio* of normality, the former is viewed as the precondition to achieving a proper understanding of the latter. Additionally, Freud dismisses the idea of the homogeneous sexual instinct implied in the degeneration theory. This was because the "composite nature" of some perversions gave Freud "a hint that perhaps the sexual instinct itself may be no simple thing, but put together from components which have come apart again in the perversions" (1905a: 162). The fact that Freud thinks of perversion in terms of the sexual instinct's perverse components, does not mean that the concept of perversion becomes an empty signifier per se. For, although Freud does indeed bid farewell to the 'classical' concept of perversion, the term perversion is retained and redefined "in its relation to the normal" (1905a: 161).

> If a perversion, instead of appearing merely *alongside* the normal sexual aim and object ... [if] it ousts them completely and takes their place in *all* circumstances – if, in short, a perversion has the characteristics of exclusiveness and fixation – then we shall usually be justified in regarding it as a pathological symptom.
>
> *(1905a: 161)*

Having reconstructed Freud's recalibration of the formal definition of perversion in contrast to that of Krafft-Ebing, we now need to explore Freud's concrete implementation of the sadistic and masochistic perversion(s). Subsequently, we will focus on what is really at stake in the *Three Essays*, i.e. the relation of these perversions to the psychoneuroses, most specifically, hysteria.

Sadism and masochism as perversion

Despite the fundamental conceptual shift with regard to the status of the perversions in general, Freud determines the content of sadism and masochism by making an almost exclusive appeal to Krafft-Ebing. It is striking, however, that Freud's attention is only directed towards those themes that play a central role in the clinic of hysteria. Thus, Freud selects those issues from Krafft-Ebing's discussion of sadism and masochism which fit with the model of psychoneurosis that is central to the *Three Essays*. In what follows, we will illustrate how the research matrix of hysteria is constitutive for Freud's elaboration of the psychoanalytical concepts of sadism and masochism.

Regarding the role of sadism and masochism, it is worth noting that they only appear at the end of the list of perversions extensively discussed by Freud. His list begins with a description of sexual inversion, in which the theory of bisexuality is mentioned for the first time. Next, Freud turns his attention to oral sexuality, focusing on the issue of disgust, and to looking and groping, focusing on the topic of shame. Freud closes his list of perversions characterized by deviations of the sexual goals with sadism and masochism. It would of course be unthinkable to ignore the perversions that Krafft-Ebing had described as the perversions par excellence. At the same time, however, it is already more than clear that aggression is not of central importance in Freud's research matrix of hysteria.

Introducing sadism and masochism, Freud immediately stresses his indebtedness to Krafft-Ebing. He states the following: "The most common and the most significant of all the perversions – the desire to inflict pain upon the sexual object, and its reverse – received from Krafft-Ebing the names of 'sadism' and 'masochism' for its active and passive forms respectively" (1905a: 157). It is striking, however, that Freud immediately and in an oversimplified way introduces sadism and masochism as active and passive variants of one and the same perversion. By so doing, Freud in fact – without any further argumentation – presents a hypothesis that was already suggested in Krafft-Ebing's later work. Like Krafft-Ebing, Freud hints that the pleasure found in pain, humiliation and subjection is the common denominator of both sadism and masochism: "Other authors [e.g. Schrenck-Notzing (1899)] have preferred the narrower term 'algolagnia'. This emphasizes the pleasure in *pain*, the cruelty; whereas the names chosen by Krafft-Ebing bring into prominence the pleasure in any form of humiliation or subjection" (1905a: 157). If pain is not the essence of sadism and masochism, their common nature has to be thought of in terms of subjection. In comparison to Krafft-Ebing, Freud makes very explicit claims concerning the unity of sadism and masochism. Nevertheless, sadism and masochism are also discussed separately in order to reach their respective pathogenic roots.

Sadism

Although sadism is conceptualized as pleasure in the humiliation of the sexual object, Freud does not refrain from simultaneously referring to it as "active algolagnia" (1905a: 157). This could suggest that pain has a much more important role to play than Freud initially wanted us to believe. Nevertheless, Freud subsequently returns to Krafft-Ebing's line of thought. He understands sadism in relation to male nature, arguing that "the roots are easy to detect in the normal" (1905a: 159). Thus, Freud continues with the following claim:

> The sexuality of most male human beings contains an element of aggressiveness – a desire to subjugate; the biological significance of it seems to lie in the need for overcoming the resistance of the sexual object by means other than the process of wooing.
>
> *(1905a: 159)*

For Freud, sadism goes back to a preliminary sexual aim, which is more or less secondary to the sexual rapprochements (*aggredi*) which are part of the play of seduction (e.g. an inviting look). This play of seduction is finally related to the seizure of the sexual object. The intensity of this seizure is directly proportional to the object's resistance to it. Nevertheless, this kind of situation cannot be called a perversion per se, because when the aforementioned aggression is accompanied by other aspects of sexual seduction, Freud is not talking about sadism in terms of perversion. For Freud, the latter only corresponds to "an aggressive component of the sexual instinct which has become independent and exaggerated and, by displacement, has usurped the leading position" (1905a: 158). Accordingly, Freud can acknowledge that the sexual instinct comprises the perverse roots of sadism. Only in those cases where the sadistic component is displayed in an isolated and excessive manner can one talk about sadism in terms of perversion.

With respect to the question concerning the origin of sadism as a component of the sexual instinct, Freud first, like Krafft-Ebing, refers to cultural history:

> The history of human civilization shows beyond any doubt that there is an intimate connection between cruelty and the sexual instinct; but nothing has been done towards explaining this connection, apart from laying emphasis on the aggressive factor in the libido.
>
> *(1905a: 159)*

Despite having denounced Krafft-Ebing's theory of degeneration, Freud still refers to the atavistic theory of sexuality which is connected to it in order to answer the question of sadism's etiology. This theory of sexuality to which Krafft-Ebing refers not only models sexuality on hunger, but also views the most archaic form of sexuality as implying the eating of the love object.

> According to some authorities, this aggressive element of the sexual instinct is in reality a relic of cannibalistic desires – that is, it is a contribution derived from the apparatus for obtaining mastery, which is concerned with the satisfaction of the other and, ontogenetically, the older of the great instinctual needs.
>
> *(1905a: 159)*

Apart from the fact that he can make use of Krafft-Ebing as an authority argument, this cannibalistic theory is *gefundeness Fressen* for Freud. The theme of cannibalism fits seamlessly with the theme of orality, which plays a central role in the clinic of hysteria.

Freud argues that the sadistic component of the sexual instinct partly goes back to an originary aggression which cannot be deduced from sexuality. This non-sexual aggression later fuses with the sexual instinct. Freud refers to the former as "the element of aggressiveness" (1905a: 160). The "apparatus for obtaining mastery" to which Freud is referring has a secondary role in sexuality and is at the service of an ontogenetically older need, i.e. the satisfaction of hunger (1905a: 159).

Masochism

Freud's elaboration of masochism is much less substantial than his treatment of sadism. Like Krafft-Ebing, Freud presents masochism as the passive counterpart of sadism. In the first two editions of the *Three Essays*, masochism is still analysed on the basis of its proper pathogenic roots. According to Freud, the mechanism of 'sexual overvaluation' has an important role to play in this context. Operating in the "psychological sphere", the latter mechanism is defined by Freud as follows:

> The subject becomes as it were, intellectually infatuated (that is, his powers of judgement are weakened) by the mental achievements and perfections of the sexual object and he submits to the latter's judgements with credulity. Thus the credulity of love becomes an important, if not the most fundamental, source of *authority*.
>
> *(1905a: 150)*

Applied to masochism, it goes: "One at least of the roots of masochism can be inferred with equal certainty. It arises from sexual overvaluation as a necessary psychical consequence of the choice of a sexual object" (1905a: 158 note 1).[4] Once again, Freud's debt to Krafft-Ebing becomes clear; the notion of 'sexual overvaluation', which is displayed in a magnified way in the condition of masochism, is remarkably congruent with Krafft-Ebing's notion of 'sexual bondage'. Contrary to Krafft-Ebing, who strictly distinguishes *geschlechtliche Hörigkeit* from perverse masochism, Freud suggests a continuity between the submissiveness of masochism and the docility of sexual overvaluation. Moreover, psychic overvaluation goes back to the issue of 'anatomical extensions', which has a central status in Freud's analysis of hysteria. When Freud explains masochism in terms of psychic overvaluation, hysteria again emerges as the guiding pathological model of his analysis. This is further corroborated by Freud's confession that he "cannot help recalling the credulous submissiveness shown by a hypnotized subject towards the hypnotist", which he links to the manifestation of "the masochistic components of the sexual instinct" (1905: 150, note 150). This allusion to hypnosis, of course, refers to Freud's former method of treating hysteric patients and acknowledges that Freud's interpretation of masochism is determined by the model of hysteria.

Sadism and masochism as one perversion

Sadism and masochism are understood by Freud as analogous to voyeurism and exhibitionism ("the perversions which are directed towards looking and being looked at"), i.e. as one perversion and as having "a very remarkable characteristic". This characteristic is explained as follows: "In these perversions the sexual aim occurs in two forms, an active and a passive one" (1905a: 157). The active-sadistic and the passive-masochistic modes of this perversion do not merely imply a theoretical unity, a construction based on similar clinical phenomena. While Krafft-Ebing was always rather reticent with respect to putting forward the simultaneous manifestation of sadism and masochism as a general rule, this is far from the case with Freud. What for Krafft-Ebing is possible in 'some cases', is conceived by Freud as a general fact. Not only are sadism and masochism the two modes of the same perversion, but, according to Freud, both modes are always articulated together: "The most remarkable feature of this perversion is that its active and passive forms are *habitually* found to occur together in the same individual" (1905a: 159; my italics). With respect to this effective unity, Freud makes an appeal to the British physician Havelock Ellis (1859–1939), who argues that "the investigation of histories of sadism and masochism, even those given by Krafft-Ebing . . . constantly reveals traces of both groups of phenomena in the same individual" (1905a: 159–160). In what specific sense, however, do we have to understand "the simultaneous presence of these opposites" (1905a: 160)?

In the first place, and analogous to Krafft-Ebing, Freud could have been thinking of the role of phantasy, enabling the sadist or the masochist to take up the opposite position. This is, Freud claims, because a "person who feels pleasure in producing pain in someone else in a sexual relationship is also capable of enjoying as pleasure any pain which he may himself derive from sexual relations" (1905a: 159). Freud does not specify to what extent the mutual convertibility of the sadistic and the masochistic position is based on phantasy, but he agrees with Krafft-Ebing that one of the two modes is the dominant one: "A sadist is always at the same time a masochist, although the active or the passive aspect of the perversion may be the more strongly developed in him and may represent his predominant sexual activity" (1905a: 159). Freud suggests that, in principle, sadism and masochism are always present simultaneously. Therefore, he again makes an appeal to Krafft-Ebing, who cautiously suggested explaining 'some of the cases' on the basis of the theory of bisexuality. Freud, however, extrapolates the hypothesis of bisexuality to all cases and, in so doing, grounds the unity of sadism and masochism. He declares that "we should rather be inclined to connect the simultaneous presence of these opposites with the opposing masculinity and femininity which are combined in bisexuality" (1905a: 160). The attractiveness of the hypothesis of bisexuality is again determined by the fact that it accords with Freud's analysis of hysteria. The hypothesis of a congenital bisexuality – which is central in his discussion of hysteria – is presented by Freud as a way to understand the unity of sadism and masochism as one perversion. This position, however, does not contribute to the further elucidation of the etiology of sadism and masochism. Hence Freud makes the following acknowledgment: "All that need be said is that no satisfactory explanation of this perversion has been put forward and that it seems possible that a number of mental impulses are combined in it to produce a single resultant" (1905a: 159). In other words, Freud has to confess that he does not manage to provide a clear etiology for sadism and masochism.

Sadism, masochism and psychoneurosis

The perverse components of the sexual instinct which, in the perverse condition, are articulated in an exclusive, magnified and direct way, can also express themselves in an alternative way. Hence, in the psychoneuroses the very same perverse components are expressed indirectly. In his *Three Essays*, however, Freud makes use of a very particular psychoneurosis in order to clarify the relation between perversions and neuroses, i.e. conversion hysteria. Before questioning the concrete manifestation of sadism and masochism in the psychoneuroses, we will briefly explain the relation between perversion and neurosis.

Freud argues that neurotic symptoms go back to the very same sexual components that become manifest in the perversions. These perverse components are:

> [t]he most important and only constant source of energy of the neurosis and . . . the sexual life of the persons in question is expressed – whether exclusively or principally or only partly – in these symptoms . . . The symptoms constitute the sexual activity of the patient.
>
> *(1905a: 163)*

The neurotic symptoms are "substitutes" of repressed perverse impulses. In conversion hysteria, this substitution finds "an expression (by means of the process of conversion) in somatic phenomena" (1905a: 164). More specifically, hysteria is the expression of a very particular sexual disposition. Hysteria's "constitutional character", i.e. "the predominant development of the sexual instinct", conflicts with the corresponding "intensification of the resistance against the sexual instinct", i.e. disgust and shame (1905a: 164–165). The neurotic symptoms are the result of these conflicts. Freud thus acknowledges that "symptoms are formed in part at the cost of abnormal sexuality; neuroses are, so to say, the negative of perversions" (1905a: 165). In the case study of Dora, Freud adds that the "unconscious *phantasies* [of psycho-neurotics] show precisely the same content as the documentarily recorded *actions* of perverts – even though they have not read Krafft-Ebing's *Psychopathia Sexualis*, to which simple-minded people attribute such a large share of responsibility for the production of perverse tendencies" (1905b: 50).

Since neurosis consists of the indirect manifestation of the repressed perverse components of the sexual instinct, this also implies that both sadistic and masochistic tendencies can be expressed in it in a neurotic way. The foregoing analysis leads to the following question: How does Freud locate sadism and masochism within his analysis of the psychoneuroses?

Component instincts

In his discussion of the psychoneuroses, Freud once again gives special attention to the sadistic and masochistic components. As in the case of the perversions, this follows in the wake of his analysis of the voyeuristic component which is of importance for the analysis of hysteric shame. Freud writes:

> An especially prominent part is played as factors in the formation of symptoms in psychoneuroses by the component instincts, which emerge for the most part as pairs of opposites and which we have met with as introducing new sexual aims – the scopophilic instinct and exhibitionism and the active and passive forms of the instinct for cruelty.
>
> *(1905a: 166)*

The importance of the voyeuristic and exhibitionistic components, referred to from now on as 'component instincts', of course makes sense given the specific research context of hysteria. As we shall see, however, it is less evident how one could attribute a similarly central role to the sadistic and masochistic component instincts in this context. That Freud, in fact, still manages to do this, suggests that he wants, at all costs, to provide a place for both components in his hysterical matrix of neurosis. Correspondingly, he rather generally states that the "contribution" made by the "passive form of the instinct for cruelty" must be interpreted as "essential to the understanding of the fact that symptoms involve *suffering*, and it almost invariably dominates a part of the patient's social behaviour" (1905a: 66). With regard to the sadistic component instinct, Freud is equally vague:

> It is also through the medium of this connection between libido and cruelty that the transformation of love into hate takes place, the transformation of affectionate into hostile impulses, which is characteristic of a great number of cases of neurosis, and indeed, it would seem, of paranoia in general.
>
> *(1905a: 166–167)*

In turn, Freud in an oversimplified way reduces an undifferentiated series of aggressive phenomena to manifestations of the sadistic component instinct.

When pointing to their respective conditions in the unconscious, Freud again stresses the unity of the sadistic and masochistic instincts:

> Whenever we find in the unconscious an instinct of this sort which is capable of being paired off with an opposite one, this second instinct will regularly

be found in operation as well. Every active perversion is thus accompanied by its passive counterpart.

(1905a: 167)

Although both component instincts are not necessarily equally powerful, they are, according to Freud, cooperating and directed towards the same goal: "In anyone who suffers from the consequences of repressed sadistic impulses there is sure to be another determinant of his symptoms which has its source in masochistic inclinations" (1905a: 167). Despite the fact that both of these different components go together in a unity, Freud reminds us that "in the actual symptoms one or another of the opposing tendencies plays the predominant part" (1905a: 167). In other words, the question concerning the unity of sadism and masochism, of them being the active and passive forms of the very same perversion, reappears in Freud's discussion of psychoneurosis.

In what follows, we argue that Freud once again tries to explain the psychoneurotic unity of sadistic and masochistic perverse tendencies by taking them back to a common origin. Freud suggests that the latter is situated in a common 'erotogenic zone'. It is necessary to elucidate this issue because, together with bisexuality, the diversity of erotogenic zones functions is the most important factor of Freud's analysis of hysteria.

Erotogenic zones

In accordance with the model of conversion hysteria, the origin of the component instincts is situated by Freud in specific bodily zones, i.e. the so-called "erotogenic zones" (1905a: 167).[5] In hysteria, these erotogenic zones are particularly susceptible to the manifestation of neurotic conversion symptoms through which the repressed component instincts can be indirectly satisfied. In the first two editions of the *Three Essays* (1905, 1910), the erotogenic zone has a prominent place in Freud's analysis of the component instincts:

> We can distinguish in them [the component instincts] (in addition to an "instinct" which is not in itself sexual and which has its source in motor impulses) a contribution from an organ capable of receiving stimuli (e.g. the skin, the mucous membrane, or a sense organ). An organ of this kind will be described in this connection as an "erotogenic zone" – as being the organ whose excitation lends the instinct a sexual character.
>
> *(1905a: 168 note 1)*

According to Freud, it is the specific "chemical nature" that determines that the respective excitation is in fact *sexual* excitation. He adds that "we speak of the organ concerned as the 'erotogenic zone' of the sexual component instinct arising from it" (1905a: 168). As such, the specific component instinct is always related to its corresponding erotogenic zone.

In the case of "those impulses which create new sexual aims and seem independent of erotogenic zones", however, the identification of a well-defined erotogenic zone is problematic (1905a: 169). Although Freud must have been aware of this difficulty, he does whatever he can to justify the research matrix of hysteria:

> The significance of the erotogenic zones as apparatuses subordinate to the genitals and as substitutes for them is, among all the psychoneuroses, most clearly to be seen in hysteria; but this does not imply that significance is any the less in the other forms of illness. It is only that in them it is less recognizable, because in their case (obsessional neurosis and paranoia) the formation of the symptoms takes place in regions of the mental apparatus which are more remote from the particular centres concerned with somatic control.
>
> *(1905a: 169)*

As we can see, Freud is doing whatever he can in order to safeguard the model of hysteria and the corresponding criterion of the erotogenic zones. Nevertheless, at the same time, it is also clear that the sadistic and masochistic component instincts are putting Freud's research matrix under pressure.

In a seemingly casual fashion, Freud declares the following: "In *obsessional neurosis* what is more striking is the significance of those impulses which create new sexual aims and *seem independent* of erotogenic zones" (1905a: 169; my italics). In the first editions of the *Three Essays* (1905, 1910), Freud adds the following idea: "[The German psychiatrist Wilhelm] Strohmayer has very rightly inferred from a case under his observation that *obsessive self-reproaches* originate from suppressed sadistic impulses" (1905a: 169, note 2; my italics). As such, Freud implicitly acknowledges that, compared to hysteria, obsessional neurosis appears to be a much more interesting pathology for getting to grips with sadism and masochism. Nevertheless, the discussion of obsessional neurosis against the backdrop of the model of hysteria hinders Freud from further elucidating the role of sadism and masochism.

Freud does whatever he can to uphold the research matrix of hysteria. Hence, he attempts to explain the unity of the paired component instincts on the basis of a common origin in the same erotogenic zone:

> Nevertheless, in scopophilia and exhibitionism the eye corresponds to an erotogenic zone; while in the case of those components of the sexual instinct which involve pain and cruelty the same role is assumed by the skin – the skin, which in particular parts of the body has become differentiated into sense organs or modified into mucous membrane, and thus is the erotogenic zone *par excellence*.
>
> *(1905a: 169)*

Freud artificially tries to connect sadism and masochism, as the active and passive form of the same perversion, to one common erotogenic zone, i.e. the skin. Nevertheless, if it is the erotogenic zone of the instinct involving pain and cruelty, the skin does not really help us in grasping the origin of the sadistic and masochistic component instincts. Moreover, the skin is also eligible to serve as the erotogenic zone of the so-called 'instinct of contrectation', which "represents a need for contact with the skin" (1905a: 169 note 2).[6] The "pleasure ... afforded by tactile sensations of the skin of the sexual object" is also mentioned by Freud in the context of his analysis of scopophilia (1905a: 156). According to Freud, scopophilia is "ultimately" derived from the very same instinct of contrectation. The latter thus shares the erotogenic zone of the skin together with the instinct involving pain and cruelty. Freud is thus capable of providing an erotogenic zone for the sadistic and masochistic component instincts, notwithstanding the fact that the respective zone is anything but specific and is shared with other component instincts. This artificial explanation does not make Freud's hypothesis any more convincing, quite the contrary. Nevertheless, Freud subsequently continues this line of reasoning in the second part of his 'triptych' on sexuality, which specifically deals with the infantile origins of adult sexuality. This means that Freud endeavours to make sadism and masochism fit into an analysis modelled on hysteria in the second essay as well.

Infantile sources of sadism and masochism

At the end of his first essay, Freud concludes "that there is indeed something innate lying behind the perversions". He adds "that it is something innate in *everyone*, though as a disposition it may vary in its intensity and may be increased by the influences of actual life. What is in question are the innate constitutional roots of the sexual instinct" (1905a: 171). Freud assumes that "this postulated constitution, containing the germs of all the perversions, will only be demonstrable in children, even though in them it is only with modest degrees of intensity that any of the instincts can emerge" (1905a: 172). We therefore need to ascertain what the status of the sadistic and masochistic components is in infantile sexuality. It soon becomes clear that the primacy of the erotogenic zones, which dominate and structure infantile sexuality, compels Freud to formulate a residual category of "certain instincts (such as the scopophilic instinct and the instinct for cruelty) of which the origin is not yet completely intelligible" (1905a: 200–201). Thus, the analysis of infantile sexuality, in turn, reveals how the research model of hysteria makes it impossible for Freud to adequately elaborate the sadistic and masochistic component instincts.

Initially and primarily, infantile sexuality was presented and explained by Freud by making an appeal to the scheme of orality and the model of the sucking of the child, or, in fact rather, the paradigm of the lips kissing themselves:

> Our study of thumb-sucking or sensual sucking has already given us the two essential characteristics of an infantile sexual manifestation. At its origin, it attaches itself to one of the vital somatic functions; it has as yet no sexual object, and is thus autoerotic; and its sexual aim is dominated by an

erotogenic zone. It is to be anticipated that these characteristics will be found to apply equally the most of the other activities of the infantile sexual instincts.

(1905a: 182–183)

The paradigmatic role of orality in Freud's analysis of infantile sexuality should in turn be contextualized with regard to the prevailing model of hysteria. Freud's presentation of an infantile sexuality, which is autoerotic and dominated by the erotogenic zones, results once more in a separate status for the sadistic and masochistic components. "It must", Freud argues, "be admitted that infantile sexual life, in spite of the preponderating dominance of erotogenic zones, exhibits components which from the very first involve other people as sexual objects" (1905a: 192). He continues with the following claim:

> Such are the instincts of scopophila, exhibitionism and cruelty, which *appear in a sense independently* of erotogenic zones; these instincts do not enter into intimate relations with genital life *until later*, but are already to be observed in childhood as independent impulses, distinct *in the first instance* from erotogenic sexual activity.
>
> (1905a: 192; my italics)

Of the two examples Freud gives, the instinct for cruelty is the more extreme: "The cruel component of the sexual instinct develops in childhood *even more independently* [than do the scopophilic and exhibitionistic components] of the sexual activities that are attached to the erotogenic zones" (1905a: 192; my italics and my addition between brackets). Freud refers to both sadism and masochism in his discussion of the instinct for cruelty and differentiates between an active (sadistic) and passive (masochistic) instinct. Nevertheless, in this discussion, Freud can again be seen to explicitly stress the sadistic instinct, thus making the active instinct for cruelty his ultimate reference point.

The active impulse for cruelty

According to Freud, the active impulse for cruelty "arises from the instinct for mastery" (1905a: 193). The latter instinct can therefore also be connected with the aforementioned "apparatus for obtaining mastery, which is concerned with the satisfaction of the other and, ontogenetically, the older of the great instinctual needs" (1905a: 159). The instinct for mastery could thus manifest itself via the apparatus for obtaining mastery and originate in "an 'instinct' which is not itself sexual and which has its source in motor impulses" (1905a: 168, note 1). This means that Freud traces the instinct for cruelty back to an instinctual force which is not derivable from sexuality, but which joins erotogenic sexuality, becoming an integral part of it. In the first two editions of the *Three Essays*, Freud articulates the following observation:

It may be assumed that the impulses of cruelty arise from sources which are in fact independent of sexuality, but may become united with it at an early stage owing to an anastomosis [cross-connection] near their points of origin. Observation teaches us, however, that sexual development and the development of the instinct of scopophilia and cruelty are subject to mutual influences which limit this presumed independence of the two sets of instincts.

(1905a: 193, note 1)

Freud presupposes a "connection between the cruel and the erotogenic instincts ... established in childhood" and simultaneously suggests that "the presumed independence" of the instinct for cruelty somehow is related to what he rather vaguely calls "mutual influences" (1905a: 193). Even if Freud is able to connect the instinct for cruelty with erotogenic sexuality, the non-specific nature of sadism's erotogenic source is again very remarkable. Freud locates this source in the skin and the muscles. In the context of oral autoerotism, e.g. when he refers to a "grasping-instinct", this is a pleasure that derives from muscular activity (1905a: 180).

Freud discusses the role of muscular activity as one of the sources of infantile sexuality: "We are all familiar with the fact that children feel a need for a large amount of active muscular exercise and derive extraordinary pleasure from satisfying it" (1905a: 202). Freud refers to children's play in terms of "romping or wrestling with playmates – a situation in which, apart from general muscular exertion, there is a large amount of contact with the skin of the opponent" (1905a: 202–203). It is during this active exercise of the muscles, Freud writes, that a large number of people for the very first time experience excitement in their genitals. The young child's expression of force, in other words, coincides with the activation of the genital erotogenic zone. In this way, the instinct for mastery is connected to erotogenic genital sexuality. It is perhaps this phenomenon which Freud has in mind when he discusses an anastomosis. The instinct for mastery, which initially is autonomous and must be distinguished from erotogenic sexuality, joins erotogenic sexuality via anastomosis and as such becomes eroticized. Musculature correspondingly becomes a source of the infantile instinct for cruelty: "One of the roots of the sadistic instinct would seem to lie in the encouragement of sexual excitation by muscular activity" (1905a: 203). It is remarkable that Freud interprets the pleasurable physical struggle of little children in terms of object-choice and from the perspective of the genital instinct's later preferences. Discussing the activation of the genital erotogenic zone, he stresses the importance of the contribution of the instinct for mastery to male sexuality (1905a: 188).

Freud holds that infantile sadism, i.e. the experience of sexual pleasure in the instinct for mastery, can develop into pleasure in cruelty because it was not stopped or damned by pity initially. "Cruelty in general comes easily to the childish nature", Freud writes, "since the obstacle that brings the instinct for mastery to a halt at another person's pain – namely a capacity for pity – is developed relatively late" (1905a: 192–193). The barrier of pity suggests an inherent aspect of perverse sadism which, given the research matrix of hysteria, cannot be articulated, namely narcissistic pleasure. This is because the constitutive precondition of pity implies an ego which can experience itself as being in a relation to an object. The sadist narcissistically enjoys the overcoming and putting aside of pity: "The absence of the barrier of pity brings with it a danger that the connection between the cruel and the erotogenic instincts, thus established in childhood, may prove unbreakable in later life" (1905a: 193). The barrier of pity is, according to this line of thought, a reaction formation which is constituted both at the cost of and as an expression of the repressed sadistic component instincts.

The passive impulse for cruelty

As was already pointed out, Freud focuses almost exclusively on sadism. When giving more information about masochism with respect to its infantile sources, like in sadism, there is no reference to any narcissistic pleasure at all. In accordance with the attention given to the erotogenic zones in the matrix of hysteria, Freud merely refers to the skin as an erotogenic source of infantile masochistic pleasure: "Ever since Jean Jacques Rousseau's *Confessions*, it has been well known to all educationists that the painful stimulation of the skin of the buttocks is one of the erotogenic roots of the *passive* instinct of cruelty (masochism)" (1905a: 193).[7] In a certain sense, this minimalistic explanation of the infantile roots of masochism is typical of Freud's *Three Essays* in that it only explicates masochism by means of a reference to sadism. Despite the fact that Freud presents sadism and masochism as two sides of the same coin, he sheds relatively little light on the masochistic side itself.

Conclusion

Krafft-Ebing introduced sadism and masochism as two of the perversions par excellence in the field of sexology. Freud went on to give them a central place in psychoanalytic metapsychology. In his *Three Essays*, however, Freud repeatedly admits that the conceptualization of sadism and masochism is rather problematic. We argued that the research matrix of hysteria prevented him from developing an adequate *formal* conceptualization of either sadism or masochism. At the same time, Freud draws his clinical information in an almost exclusive but selective fashion from Krafft-Ebing. To put it differently, Freud limits himself to the information in Krafft-Ebing that is compatible with the model of hysteria central to his own thinking. Indeed, Freud goes one step further than Krafft-Ebing in maintaining that the unity of sadism and masochism is a general rule. By doing so, he influences a whole generation of psychoanalysts after him. Although he rarely mentions the term himself, Freud is in fact responsible for the ubiquitous coupling of sadism and masochism into the single term 'sadomasochism'. More than Krafft-Ebing, Freud thus is defending this unity's simultaneous gratification of sadism and masochism.

The research matrix of hysteria that is central to the *Three Essays* – a matrix in which both the erotogenic zones and the issue of bisexuality are essential elements – leads Freud to an inadequate conceptualization of human aggression in terms of sadism and masochism. Nevertheless, this conceptualization remains problematic later in his career as well. The most successful attempt to articulate the essence of both sadism and masochism perhaps can be found in his meta-psychological papers, particularly 'The Instincts and their Vicissitudes' (Freud 1915) and 'Mourning and Melancholia' (Freud 1917). Moreover, until 'A Child is Being Beaten' (Freud 1919) Freud defends the primacy of sadism in relation to masochism. This situation changes in 'Beyond the Pleasure Principle' (Freud 1920) and 'The Economic Problem of Masochism' (Freud 1924), where Freud introduces the idea of a primary masochism. The de facto equalization of sadism and masochism, as complementary manifestations of the death instinct, only contributes further to the use of sadism and masochism as passe-partout concepts that are too oversimplified for comprehending the theme of human aggression.

Notes

1 In what follows, the German concept of *Trieb* will henceforth be translated as 'instinct', in accordance with the English translation of both Krafft-Ebing's and Freud's work. On this issue, see Herman Westerink's contribution in this volume.
2 For the link between the phenomena of flagellation and masochism in sexology and psychoanalysis, see Vandermeersch (2002: 221–248).
3 For a reconstruction of the history of the idea of original bisexuality, see Angelides (2001).
4 This fragment is omitted from the 1915 edition onwards. In this and the subsequent editions of the text, masochism is presented by Freud as a by-product of sadism. This shift in the conceptualization of masochism goes together with Freud's tendency to focus on obsessional neurosis – instead of hysteria – as the central research matrix, as can be illustrated in his meta-psychological study 'Instincts and their Vicissitudes' (Freud 1915). See De Vleminck (2013).
5 Freud became acquainted with the concept of the 'erotogenic zone' from Krafft-Ebings's *Psychopathia Sexualis*. Nevertheless, he rules out the original, exclusive link between the erotogenic zones and the genitals, which is still present in Krafft-Ebing (1903: 24). Freud first mentions the erotogenic zones in the context of his research on hysteria. He writes: "Erotogenic and hysterogenic zones show the same characteristics" (Freud 1905a: 184).
6 Freud is acquainted with this 'instinct of contrectation' via the German psychiatrist and sexologist Albert Moll and his *Untersuchungen über der Libido Sexualis* (Moll 1898). See Harry Oosterhuis' chapter in this volume.
7 Freud has this reference from Krafft-Ebing (1903: 110–111).

References

American Psychiatric Association (2013). *Diagnostic and Statistical Manual of Mental Disorders, 5th Edition: DSM-5*. Washington, DC and London: American Psychiatric Publishing.
Angelides, S. (2001). *A History of Bisexuality*. Chicago, IL and London: University of Chicago Press.
Davidson, A.I. (1987). How to do the History of Psychoanalysis: A Reading of Freud's "Three Essays on the Theory of Sexuality". *Critical Inquiry* 13:2, 252–277.
De Vleminck, J. (2013). *De schaduw van Kaïn: Freuds klinische antropologie van de agressiviteit* [*The Shadow of Cain: Freud's Clinical Anthropology of Aggression*]. Leuven: Leuven University Press.

Ellenberger, H. (1970). *The Discovery of the Unconscious: The History and Evolution of Dynamic Psychiatry*. New York: Basic Books.
Freud, S. (1905a). *Three Essays on the Theory of Sexuality*. J. Strachey (ed.), *Standard Edition 7*. London: Hogarth.
Freud, S. (1905b). Fragment of an Analysis of a Case of Hysteria, *SE 7*.
Freud, S. (1915). Instincts and Their Vicissitudes. *SE 14*.
Freud, S. (1917). Mourning and Melancholia. *SE 17*.
Freud, S. (1919). A Child is Being Beaten. *SE 17*.
Freud, S. (1920). *Beyond the Pleasure Principle*. *SE 18*.
Freud, S. (1924). The Economic Problem of Masochism. *SE 19*.
Krafft-Ebing, R. von (1903). *Psychopathia Sexualis: With Especial Reference to the Antipathic Sexual Instinct: A Medico-Forensic Study*. Transl. F.S. Klaf, New York: Arcade, 1965.
Moll, A. (1898). *Untersuchungen über die Libido sexualis*. Berlin: Fischer's Medicinische Buchhandlung/H. Kornfeld.
Oosterhuis, H. (2000). *Stepchildren of Nature: Krafft-Ebing, Psychiatry, and the Making of Sexual Identity*. Chicago and London: The University of Chicago Press.
Porter, R. (2002). *Madness: A Brief History*. New York: Oxford University Press.
Sulloway, F.J. (1979). *Freud, Biologist of the Mind: Beyond the Psychoanalytic Legend*. New York: Basic Books.
Vandermeersch, P. (2002). *La chair de la passion: Une histoire de foi: la flagellation*. Paris: Cerf.
Van Haute, P & Geyskens, T. (2012). *A Non-Oedipal Psychoanalysis? A Clinical Anthropology of Hysteria in the Works of Freud and Lacan*. Leuven: Leuven University Press.

6

VARIATIONS, COMPONENTS AND ACCIDENTS

Critical reflections on Freud's concept of the drive

Monique David-Ménard

Many traps await the reader of a canonical text. A clear example of this can be found in the polemic between Foucault and Derrida concerning Descartes' *Meditations on First Philosophy*. This debate concerns Descartes' claim that he cannot conceive of the sequence 'I doubt, I am, I exist' while himself being mad. It is worth recalling the crucial sentence: "Mais quoi, ce sont des fous et je ne serais pas moins extravagant si je me réglais sur leur exemple" (Descartes 1967 [1641]: 406)! Should we follow Foucault and maintain that this sentence expresses the *Grand renfermement* of madness (Foucault 1972), or should we follow Derrida who asserts that Descartes' gesture here is a traditional one: philosophy confronts the possibility of madness and detaches itself from it (Derrida 1967: 51–98)? The answer depends on the resolution of another question: is the text sufficiently unified for the answer itself to be ascertained? Moreover, in a psychoanalytic reading of texts, the question is even more complicated because it always refers those texts to clinical observations. Does Freud express himself in the same way when he elaborates the concept of drive and when he speaks of the Dora case study? One question leads to another: what do we retain from Freud to understand our clinical work? How do we address the difference between a clinical and a conceptual perspective, when, already in Freud's day, differences in clinical and conceptual vocabulary reflect differences in thinking?

Breaking with dualities to understand the sexual

While writing *L'hysterique entre Freud et Lacan* (David-Ménard 1983, 2014), I became aware immediately that theoretical language, stuck in dualities that are hardly recognizable, can lack the clarity of the clinical texts of Freud and other authors, especially those of Karl Landauer (1926). Landauer's definition of the body reduces it neither to linguistic phenomena (even if conversion replaces repressed sentences) nor to physiological phenomena. As early as the *Studies in Hysteria*, Freud makes reference to the legs of Elisabeth von R., which are said to have joined in the conversation during the treatment (Freud 1895: 148). This expression and the very idea of a corporeal language would make no sense in a dualist model of the drives. Nonetheless, in the 1915 edition of the *Three Essays*, Freud comments that the drive is "a concept that defines the frontier between the mental and the physical" (Freud 1905: 168). Freud states that:

> [a]n "instinct" appears to us as a concept on the frontier between the mental and the somatic, as the psychical representative of the stimuli originating from within the organism and reaching the mind, as a measure of the demand made upon the mind for work in consequence of its connection with the body.
>
> *(Freud 1915: 121–122)*

This definition of the relation between body and soul is anything but clear. It simultaneously highlights and dismisses the need to make a distinction between the body and the soul. In this text, and once again in a lecture from 1932, Freud recognizes the obscure and provisional nature of these expressions (Freud 1933). What is focused on in 1915 is the notion of 'excitation' relative to a demand made upon the psychical apparatus. The drive is frequently said to excite the psyche, even if the concept of 'excitation' is typically reserved for the physiology of the nervous system. Certainly, Freud explicitly deflects – and not without humour – the meaning of the term 'excitation' in order to define the drive. He does so in a way that makes one wonder whether 'soul' means anything more for him than the decision to use the term 'excitation' in such a way that its meaning cannot be reduced to nervous physiology.

This explains why the inflation in psychoanalytic thought of the notion of the 'psychic' lacks rigour. It suggests that the difficulties linked to the concept of drive have been resolved. But Freud never pretended that this was the case. He also did not need such a resolution to make progress in his work, because what counted for him above all was the idea of the *plasticity* of the drive. This plasticity disconnects the notion of the drive from any reference to a pre-given nature. But the price paid for this development is a certain ambiguity of the notion of a pulsional destiny – a destiny founded in the dynamics of the drive – with regard to the Aristotelian, Cartesian and Spinozist notions of the body, the soul and the spirit. The equivalence of *die Seele* and *das Psychische* in Freud's thinking also bears witness to the unresolved status of this philosophical problem. Nevertheless, the value of the implementation of the concept of plasticity is that it allows us to understand and think through the transformations that define the drive. In this respect, it is decisive to compare the *Three Essays* to a later lecture from 1932, 'Anxiety and Instinctual Life'. In this text, Freud shows that the psychic does not exist in itself. It is only one of the terms that is required by his definition of the drive: "on the path from its source to its aim the instinct becomes operative psychically" (Freud 1933: 22, 96). 'Psychic' here denotes that which is active in the drive trajectory.

Immediately afterwards, in the same text, 'psychic' is reformulated in terms of energy. Obviously, the concept of drive could be developed in a much more satisfactory way if we would just leave behind the terms 'psychic' and 'somatic'.

In *Body and Language in Psychoanalysis* (David-Ménard 2014) I show in what way dualities can blur our understanding of the sexual. In fact, what Freud from 1905 onwards calls 'the erogenous body' is a quite specific reality that takes its origin from a regional epistemology; hysterical symptoms are the material element of a language in which the body, without leaving its physiological reality behind, sustains another kind of reality which Freud calls the 'hysterogenous zone'. The body of pleasure, displeasure and anxiety is not attributed to the individual closed in on him or herself. On the contrary, ever since 1895 Freud considered this dimension of erogeneity to be opened up by the traces that come from the other (*Nebenmensch*) (Freud 1950 [1895]). However, erogeneity can be reduced neither to physiology nor to the signifier.

The autonomy given to another body than the physiological one, had to establish its credibility in the face of strong objections. From a Lacanian perspective, for instance, it might be deemed impertinent to assign a reality of its own to this pulsional (plastic) body that is capable of language, because its manifestations address an other or a group of others, without at the same time being reducible to the significance of desire. The body was confined to the realm of the imaginary and to illusions of completeness, without being in any way independent from the chain of signifiers. To maintain such independence would mean, in light of the theory, that one did not leave the perspective of the symptom.

In *Body and Language in Psychoanalysis* (David-Ménard 2014) I wanted to introduce another perspective. It is not because a hysteric is in relation with an other person – an other whose presence is realized as a hallucination acted out by the body – that the demand and desire can be confined to the imaginary, or to the sign as opposed to the signifier.[1] In certain texts by Lacan, such as 'Agency of the Letter in the Unconscious, or Reason since Freud' from 1957 (Lacan 1966), there seems to be a reductive tendency that only allows for a choice between a naturalist 'figurative semiology' and a system of writing. Even if analysts of the first generation did not always find adequate concepts, they did notice that the scenarios of sexual satisfaction that the symptoms (re-)present receive their importance from the fact that these scenarios were attempts to express what was inexpressible in an original scene. In 1909, when Freud speaks of the "pantomime of satisfaction", he does so without any reference to an ideal of a 'natural expression' (Freud 1909: 229). As for Karl Landauer, he shows how agitation in children (*die kindliche Bewegungsunruhe*) can indicate a sexual drive looking for its objects and for ways to reach them, while at the same time failing to find them. Nowadays, we use Ritalin too often for turbulent children, thus preventing the organization of their drive circuits. The first analysts, on the other hand, adopted the term *Darstellung* to denote the representation of the irrepresentable that is expressed in hysterical symptoms, in psychotic anxieties and more generally in all symptoms that participate in what Freud describes as the "seed of hysteria regularly embedded in the foundation of neurosis".

Freud notes in his study on the Wolf Man: "At last, I recognized the importance of the intestinal trouble for my purposes; it represented the small trait of hysteria which is regularly to be found at the root of an obsessional neurosis" (Freud 1918: 75). This term refers to the terrain on which sexuality, always in close relation to traumatic experiences, is constituted. In Lacanian terms, the *Darstellung*, first found in hysteria and dreams, concerns the real and not only the imaginary. If we consider the scope of this epistemological remark, we move away not only from Oedipal conceptions of the sexual but also from psychological and metaphysical conceptions, even those Freud himself uses every now and then.

Variability as constitutional of the drive

At the beginning of Freud's 1905 book, *Three Essays on the Theory of Sexuality*, the drive is defined by two components, the aim and the object. At the end of the same text, the definition is changed so that it now comprises four components: the pressure, the aim, the source and the object. This change provides a new signification to the drive and to sexuality:

> I shall at this point introduce two technical terms. Let us call the person from whom sexual attraction proceeds the *sexual object* (*geschlechtliche Anziehung*) and the act towards which the instinct tends the *sexual aim* (*Sexualziel*). Scientifically sifted observation, then, shows that numerous deviations occur in respect of both of these – the sexual object and the sexual aim. The relation between these deviations and what is assumed to be normal requires thorough investigation.
>
> *(Freud 1905: 135–136)*

Sexuality is mentioned twice in this short citation. First, in reference to the difference between the sexes (*Geschlecht*), that is, to the idea of a total person as the source of a (sexual) desire for love. Second, by the use of the term *sexual* that implies no such reference. At the same time, Freud indicates that the occurrence of a large number of 'deviations' regarding the aim as well as the object of the drive – for example, when a man takes the woman's place in 'sexual inversion', or when an animal is taken as a sexual object – force us to change our understanding of drive and sexuality. Indeed, in the context of these 'deviations', the search for pleasure and for the object is no longer linked to the role of the differences between the sexes in procreation. But this argument, which invokes the reality of perversions, only suggests a modification of the concept of drive. What imposes this modification is not the mere existence of the perversions, but rather the hypothesis that neurotic symptoms (that are put in relation to sexual memories in the cure) and perversions are intrinsically linked. "The sexual instinct of psychoneurotics exhibits all the aberrations which we have studied as variations (*Variationen*) of normal, and as manifestations of abnormal, sexual life" (Freud 1905: 166). Only by reuniting so-called normal transformations with pathological transformations does the concept of variability become the organizing factor of the components of the drive. Or, rather, this reunification of the normal and the pathological relies on the observation (which is guided by the concept of the drive that is redefined in the process) that the transformations of the drive are of the same kind in normal persons, neurotics and perverts. Variability is first referred to as a 'deviation'. It designates two things. The first is the modification of the investigator's thinking, which departs from an older conception of drive to create a new concept. The second is the intrinsic character of the drive as sexual: the drive is organized by its transformations, which have their own rules and intelligibility. In the end, the establishment of multiple bridges between the pathological and the normal leads to the disappearance of an age-old common definition of drive in which sexuality and reproduction were intrinsically linked, and to its replacement by the concept of the variability of the field of the drives.

We have said that when Freud talks of 'deviations (*Abweichungen*) of aim and object', he is working towards a modification of the definition of the drive. From this perspective, the variability of the drive first and foremost concerns the variability of its components. This implies that Freud also modifies the biological use of the very notion of variability and variation in the Evolution Theory. To do so, he makes a theoretical link between two factual elements. On the one hand, neurotic symptoms lead patients to sexual memories, which are immobilized in typical scenes that include details about places, circumstances and striking details. On the other, the activities of pervert subjects present paradoxical but instructive modifications of both the object and aim of the drive. One can, for example, think of an intense pleasure that is limited to seeing and being seen – in other words, a pleasure that invests the eye and the gaze as if it were a genital organ. At the same time, however, through this substitution of the object the pleasurable experience is no longer linked in any way with procreation.

Whenever Freud writes on the variability of the objects of the drives, he gives an important role to the fetish that introduces a blockage of that same variability. If the object is a shoe, it absorbs and monopolizes sexual desire. As a result, it cannot be replaced by anything else. This monopoly is what Freud called the overvaluation of the object (1905: 150–151). He considers passion that is not directed towards an object that is usually without sexual signification, but towards a person, to be the normal equivalent of this overvaluation. Freud nevertheless hypothesizes that also in passion – and despite appearances – the drive is triggered by 'something' in the person that leads the subject, despite itself, to overestimate another person's value. However, the confrontation with something in or of the other that can trigger and satisfy the subject's desire also reveals the subject to itself. The inevitably partial character of the drive modifies the idea that the attraction finds its origin in another person. The notion of a partial drive can then definitely be established by linking what sexologists call 'perversions' (which are redefined in light of the fixity and strangeness of the object as it appears in fetishism) with the drive of ordinary passion.

The source of the drive is affirmed along with the partial character of the drive. It is not the body as a whole which is attracted, but only part of it. The notion of 'organ-pleasure' reminds us that this part is a corporeal zone that can no longer be reduced to its physiological exchanges. This notion, which Freud constantly uses to refer to the sexual character of the drive, paradoxically indicates that the sexual drive is stripped of its reproductive and physiological functions. Consequently, and from a psychoanalytic point of view, even genitalia are qualified as sexual because of the pleasure they procure and on account of their erotogenic value, not for their reproductive function. This term also underscores that it is the drive which permits us to understand otherness. Organ-pleasure implies a hallucinatory quality even when there is an object for the drive for which not only the thumb but also the breast can be taken as an example. The question of the otherness of the object and its ability to satisfy the drive is thus linked from the outset to the question of how the subject of pleasure and displeasure can leave behind autoerotism and hallucinatory satisfaction. The otherness of the object can only be represented from the perspective of the loss of a first (*earlier, primordial*) satisfaction. As Freud writes in his 1925 article 'Negation', the instauration of the reality principle is only possible through the experience that objects that once brought real satisfaction have been lost (Freud 1925: 238).

The notion of organ-pleasure makes it impossible to consider sexuality in terms of a dualistic opposition between physiology and the (morality of) love. The physiological is indeed not the domain in which a destiny can be constructed; rather the latter is a question of the organization of the drives which plays out in an erogenous body. The combination of the components (pressure, aim, object and source) defines this organization, and it is the transformation of these components that constructs destiny. The term 'destiny' is less commented upon in psychoanalytic literature than the other aspects of the drive. It is nevertheless decisive: it indicates that what is played out in the drives is intrinsically human in that it produces singular human beings whereas, at the same time, the drive also appears to be anonymous and a-subjective because its components escape the individual subjected to them.

Destiny is what escapes us. It is nonetheless a temporal reality, organized by the variability of the drives and its laws. For example: the transformation of a passive aim into an active aim, the substitution or fixation of objects, the connections between erogenous zones, or 'displacements of erogeneity', as Freud says in reference to Dora's mouth. All these processes constitute a sort of grammar of the drives. But it is only a *kind* of grammar. Even though the replaceable character of the objects of the drive and the aforementioned types of transformations put the drive at the centre of symbolic phenomena, the drive itself nevertheless resists language.

And yet these transformations are not natural either. The relations between their components are equivalent to the laws that govern the formation of the sequences of images in our dreams. Freud describes these laws in his *Interpretation of Dreams* (Freud 1900): condensation, displacement, indifference towards contradictions, plurifunctional importance of juxtaposition, etc. These laws constitute, says Freud, the work of the dream. The transformations of the drive are equivalent to this dream work, even if they concern unconscious phenomena that are closer to the acts through which our desires try to attain pleasure than to the images of the dream.

Variability and plasticity

The drive is a festival of plasticity. With regard to the drive, in 1905 Freud speaks of inversion (*Umsetzung*), of conversion (*Umwandlung*), of the sexual use of mucus membranes (*sexuelle Verwendung der Lippen-Mundschleimhaut*), of *Ersatz* objects (*ungeeigneter Ersatz des Sexualobjektes*) in fetishism, and of the invention of 'new sexual aims' for the drive in general. When Freud reiterates the acquisitions of drive theory in the lecture on anxiety and instinctual life (1932), he uses no fewer than ten terms to characterize the plasticity of drive components: some concern the aim, others the source, still others the object (Freud 1933: 97–98). The repression and modification of the aim are designated by the verbs 'deviate' (*ablenken*) and 'employ' (*verwenden*). One kind of drive satisfaction can be replaced by another (*ersetzt werden*), and this includes the possibility of renunciation (*Verzicht*), which transforms sexual desire into tenderness. It is well worth considering transpositions (*Abänderung*) and modifications (*Modifikation*) of the aim. Plasticity includes substitutability (*Vertretbarkeit*), adjournment (*Aufschiebbarkeit*), the inhibition of the aim (*zielgehemmte Triebe*), and so forth.

Up to this point we have mainly evoked three of the components that modify the common, pre-Freudian definition of drive: the object (in relation to the partial character of the drive), the source and the aim. But there is still a fourth component: pressure (*Drang*). Pressure denotes the quantity of work needed to transform the components of the drive. Concerning this notion of work, Freud's first reference is to Helmholtz and thermodynamics. But the drive cannot be explained in terms of a purely physical or physiological system. Even if we can say that a body can be analysed on a physiological level, this does not mean that the drive and the physiological functions can be unified conceptually.

Freud explains in 'Instincts and Their Vicissitudes' that the drive is a 'piece of activity' in so far as it is a constant pressure (Freud 1915: 122). The idea of an 'activity' and more precisely of a 'constant activity' is crucial and requires further clarification. First, it is necessary to clarify how it was introduced. Before being presented as one of the components of the drive, and before being turned into a noun, the idea of activity was already discretely used as a verb in the first pages of the *Three Essays*. At the beginning of the *Three Essays*, Freud describes how someone predisposed to hysteria may react in the following terms when faced with the demands of a real sexual situation: "between the pressure of the instinct (*Zwischen dem Drängen des Triebs*) and his antagonism to sexuality, illness offers him a way of escape" (Freud 1905: 165). The verb *treiben* (from which the noun *Trieb* is derived), is just as common in German as the verb *drängen*, which Freud uses (when speaking of the formation of symptoms) to refer to *that which pushes forward in the drive*, in the sense of an activity or, possibly, a constraint.

The concept of pressure is more explicitly developed in 1915 than it was in 1905. Freud even mentions it as the first of the components and as the "very essence of the drive" (Freud 1915: 122). We are the system and the destiny of our drives by virtue of this pressure, which stays active even when the aim of the drive is passive (being seen or suffering, for example). Its importance lies in its constancy. It remains unchanged while the other components are variable. To have a destiny, the drive must be animated by pressure. This constancy of the drive may evoke the *conatus* of Spinoza, which constitutes the essence of every modus, including the modus human being (Spinoza 1996 [1677]: III, prop. 6, 7). We mentioned already that for Freud the drive is a constant 'piece of activity'. This activity shares the ambiguity that also characterizes the German word *Lust*: it simultaneously indicates desire (the movement towards pleasure) and pleasure (as the aim of this movement). In this context 'pressure' (*Drang*) refers to an active force targeting pleasure while organizing complex, sinuous and even dangerous paths to its realization. Freud repeatedly clarifies the importance of this constancy by comparing the drive to an internal danger from which we cannot escape. The different ways in which the 'pressure' of the drive is characterized ('piece of activity', quantity of work required . . .) are significant because they indicate its temporal paradox. The pressure of the drive is always present in the subject and it is submitted to the transformations which structure and punctuate its existence, well below what it can master of itself. This 'piece of activity' that is the drive organizes itself in scenarios that determine the subject long before it can recognize them as their own. The pressure of the drive constitutes a monotony that is itself linked to the monotony of the aim of the drive which is to realize satisfaction by discharging all the quantities of energy stored in the apparatus of the soul. Thus, the drive is without qualities. What specifies the different drives are the transformations of aim, object and source. But since the pressure is always constant and the aim is always satisfaction through discharge – even if the latter can be reached through different means – it is also possible to define the drive in exclusively energetic terms. This idea indicates, right from the start, a link between the drive and the risk of auto-annihilation, which was affirmed very early on by Freud and which he re-examined in 1920 in the context of his work on the death instinct (Freud 1920a).

'Accidental factors' characterizing the sexual

But even in his most biological speculations Freud characterizes sexuality through 'accidental factors'. In the 1914 preface to the *Three Essays*, Freud insists that 'accidental factors' characterize the sexual:

> Throughout the entire work the various factors are placed in a particular order of precedence: preference is given to the accidental factors while disposition is left in the background, and more weight is attached to ontogenesis than to phylogenesis. For it is the accidental factors that play the principal part in analysis: they are almost entirely subject to its influence.

> The dispositional ones only come to light after them, as something stirred into activity by experience: adequate consideration of them would lead far beyond the sphere of psycho-analysis.
>
> *(Freud 1905: 131)*

This is Freud's permanent position, but what does it mean exactly? In 1920 Freud draws a parallel between the continuation of human existence through accidental sexual encounters and the biological renewal of cells through fusion with other living cells which postpones the death of every one of them. In line with his refusal to assimilate sexuality into reproduction, Freud emphasizes that it is not a matter here of producing new cells, but rather of the chemical transformation of each cell which encounters another cell. Thus, each cell is revitalized. The death instinct appears as the impossibility of profiting from these chance encounters, as a defence of narcissistic integrity.

Freud never simply identifies the drive with biological life. Even when he plays with the idea of a great cosmological synthesis, he uses the occasion to elucidate certain psychoanalytic characteristics of the drive. Proof of this can be seen in the theme of the object as it appears in 'Beyond the Pleasure Principle':

> We have already heard that conjugation, too, the temporary coalescence of two unicellular organisms, has a life-preserving rejuvenating effect of both of them. Accordingly we might attempt to apply the libido theory which has been arrived at in psychoanalysis to the mutual relationships of cells. We might suppose that the life instincts which are active in each cell takes the other cells as their objects, that they partially neutralize them (that is the process set up by them) in those cells and thus preserve their life; while the other cells do the same for them, still others sacrifice themselves in the performance of the libidinal function.
>
> *(Freud 1920a: 50)*

Freud there claims that the sexual drive neutralizes the death instinct in other cells by taking them as its object. This is not a biological theory of cellular exchanges. On the contrary, the idea of 'taking other cells as its object' characterizes the very invention of the drive. In order to fight auto-destruction, the drive invents the object (the exterior, the other . . .), which can become the target of aggression or the origin of a threat. We must remember that Freud considers the drive to be an excitation which cannot be evaded and which exhibits a constant pressure. This first opposition of interior and exterior does not exclude another interaction between these terms. In masochism, the object, the one that causes suffering, constitutes an actual invention of the other in the realm of the drive. Inventing an object that would cause suffering is a way of pitting sexuality against self-destruction. It does not mean that the other must be a whole or complete person. This last clarification allows us to go back to the first theory of drive from 1905. Freud affirmed in the *Three Essays* that the object is the most variable element of the drive and that it is not linked to it from the very start because the drive can become autoerotic (Freud 1915: 123). The object inserts itself between the source and the aim, thereby allowing satisfaction. This does not contradict the idea that the object, which is eminently substitutable, is an invention. The exterior, that is to say the other, is one of the inventions of the sexual drive that, by projection, transforms its own self-destructive tendencies. The price to pay for this detour that sexualizes the death instinct is, of course, anxiety. It is for this reason that one of the chapters from 'New Introductory Lectures' bears the title, 'Anxiety and Instinctual Life' (Freud 1933). Anxiety consists of inventing an object that would be external, in order to avoid being the prey of 'death as a result of life'.

Displacements of erogeneity: a discussion with Judith Butler on the drive in Freud

In *Body and Language in Psychoanalysis* (David-Ménard 2014), I criticized the mysterious and confusing notion of 'displacements of erogeneity' (*Libidoverschiebungen*) in Freud's work (Freud 1895). The formation of hysterical symptoms allows us to understand the formation of the erogenous body, of which genitality is only one mode. The reference, in the sessions, to an other (Elizabeth von R. and her legs; Dora and the sensation of pressure on her thorax) shows us that, with regard to the formation of so-called conversion symptoms, nothing is displaced. Rather, it is the traumatic history of our relations with 'first others', which are both close and disturbing, that tries to take shape in hysteria. Freud speaks of 'genitalization' with regard to Dora's cough and Feldmann characterizes a case of blushing as a 'genitalization of the nose' (Feldman 1922: 14 ff). In this way, both Freud and Feldmann seem to take the erection of the penis as the model and the norm of all erogenous experience. However, the history of a subject can only be understood as the formation of erogenous zones in their intrinsic relation to significant others. In this regard, Judith Butler provides an interesting reading of Freud's work (Butler 1983: 57–91). Butler is quite correct to draw attention to the confusing character of the notion of erogenous displacement. She also rightly points out that the expression 'the organs become genitalized' continues to privilege genital sexuality. This indicates at the same time the implicit heteronormativity of certain psychoanalytic texts (Butler 1983: 77).

Still, there is a subtle difference between what Freud wrote in German and what Butler dismisses all too quickly as incoherent in the translations of Freud's writings to which she refers. The English language does not enable one to draw a distinction between *connaissance* (*Erkenntnis*) and *savoir* (*Wissen*): one word, *knowledge*, is used for both notions. The fact that within cognitive theory *Erkenntnis* is with increasing frequency translated as 'cognition' does not make things any easier. The term 'cognition' is omnipresent in English and American philosophical texts, and Butler uses it very often in *Bodies that Matter* (Butler 1983). Yet the erogenous body is never constituted through *cognition*.

Butler asks whether Freud associates hypochondria with a physical pain that is subsequently invested by the search for knowledge (*visée de connaissance*), or whether it is precisely this search for knowledge that makes the combination of pleasure and pain in the erection of the penis interesting – the anxiety concerning sick organs furthering this interest (Butler 1983: 57). And she wonders how to understand this 'idea' of a sick body that pervades the whole field of the erogenous body using phallic experience as its model. Is it the idea that creates the shape of the organs? Butler further wonders whether or not Lacan's idea of the body as belonging to the imaginary, and Freud's idea of the Ego as a projection of the surface of the body imply that they subscribe to a form of idealism.

Instead of conceiving the erogenous body as the history of a fantasy that is never of the order of 'knowledge' (*Erkenntnis*) (despite its seeming so in cases of hypochondria), Butler builds her argument exclusively on the notion of 'knowledge – cognition' without taking into account the distinction between 'knowledge' (*Erkenntnis*) and 'fantasmatic knowledge' (*savoir fantasmatique*). This leads Butler to reveal ambiguities in Freud's oeuvre in a way that can almost be qualified as incoherent. She claims that we never really know whether the hypochondriacal investment of pain (or of its phallic equivalent) is preceded by a physiological moment of the 'painfully affected organ' that subsequently monopolizes the cognitive attention of the subject or if, on the contrary, this cognitive attention is awakened by the fantasmatical interest in certain parts of the body. When Freud invokes these displacements, Butler claims, we never know, epistemologically, whether they concern a real or an imaginary body, though they always privilege a phallic experience (Butler 1983: 59–61).

But another perspective can be envisioned. While Freud certainly has trouble getting away from the psychic-somatic dualism in his theoretical work, when it comes to his clinical work the question of erogeneity is addressed differently. In the clinical work there is no theoretically construed initial organic moment that is *secondarily* invested by a cognitive interest. Instead there is only what I would call the continued life (*la vie continuée*) of the erogenous body, which is repeated in the conditions of the cure. As Freud has said concerning Elisabeth von R's abasia, her legs "join in the conversation" (Freud 1895: 148).

Just as Lacan, Judith Butler criticizes the supposedly epistemological independence of the erogenous body, but she does so for different reasons. For Lacan the body is an imaginary formation, not in the sense of a philosophical idealism, but in the sense that it is linked to the Ego's dream of its own completeness. The 'objective' relation to reality ('knowledge') remains dependent on this illusion of completeness. The fantasy refers to the unconscious knowledge ('savoir') of the subject that, unwittingly, refigures its own incompleteness over and over again.

Butler for her part adopts a double position. On the one hand, she affirms that the displacements and substitutions that Freud attributes to the erogenous body concern only internal ambiguities and uncertainties in the Freudian text itself. This text vacillates between the materiality of the body and the idea of the body. On the other, the insight that an *idea* of the body is capable of producing the 'shape' of the body is not without interest for Butler. She wants to prove how an idea – and gender norms are ideas transmitted by habit and performative reiteration – can shape the bodies themselves as sexual (Butler 1983: 61). From this point of view, the Freudian sequence that links pain to the experience of the erogeneity of the penis and further to narcissism and the idea of the Ego illustrates the phallic character of the gender norms that rule the organization of society and of knowledge (cognition). Performativity here plays the role assumed by fantasy in the preceding perspectives; an idea does not really need to be (objectively) 'known' as such in order to produce gender difference.

I suggested that the privilege given to phallocentrism (and narcissism) is less general in Freud's text than Butler claims (David-Ménard 2009). In 'Instincts and Their Vicissitudes' (Freud 1915), which Freud published a year after his study on narcissism, it is not the model of phallic experience in its relation to hypochondria that prevails. In this later text, Freud time and again renounces the normative language of the genitalization of the organs that seems to give genital sexuality the role of model and origin, despite the fact that the importance given to polymorphous perverse (infantile) sexuality and to the avatars of this infantile sexuality in so-called adult sexuality clearly contradicts this reduction. Hence it is true that the 'erogenous displacements' characterize the sexual as such.

Comparing Freud's original German text on the plasticity of the drive to Butler's English text on the same topic reveals a surprising reduction. In the English text, all transformations are indeed rendered as 'substitutions'. This term covers up many distinct questions. It concerns the replacement of one erogenous zone by another; it also concerns the replacement of the idea of the body by the body itself that is organized through this idea, or, conversely, the replacement of a real pain by its idea. However, in Freud's text all forms of replacement are distinct: *Verschiebungen* and *Verdichtungen* in the dream work, but *Ersatzobjekte* in the work of mourning and, last but not least, *Übertragung* when it concerns the transposition of the drive in the space of the psychoanalytic treatment.

Conclusion

Why focus my reading of the *Three Essays* on epistemological issues that seem far removed from the question of how psychoanalysis, in its social practice and field of research, has become largely normative and reactionary within our society? It is the misrecognition of the inadequacy of Freud's basic concepts for the articulation of what he wanted to think that has engendered the 'tragic destiny' of psychoanalysis. We could say that Freud's work is half-baked. He repeatedly inaugurates new concepts to confront new phenomena and to describe the new field he was creating. At the same time, and in particular in his choice of a conceptual opposition between the somatic to the psychic, he has been unfaithful to his own theoretical effort. This, after all, consisted in freeing himself from the terminology that characterizes the discourse of psychologists, moralists, doctors and theologians. The question of different versions of the *Three Essays* is no doubt one of the aspects of the internal tension that has led psychoanalysis to normalize the sexual. But this is only one aspect. If it were the debate between constitution/variation and the unification of psychological development under the watch of Oedipus, which were the principal aspect of this normalization of psychoanalysis, why then did Freud continually affirm, for example in 1920 in 'Psychogenesis of a Case of Female Homosexuality' (Freud 1920b), that homosexuality is not a sickness? And along the same lines, why did he continually affirm that psychoanalysis does not redefine the masculine and the feminine, but instead interprets these representations on the level of the individual subject and 'puts them to work'? I agree that the concepts have political importance, but I do not agree that the alternative – constitution versus Oedipal object – has been the principal vector in promoting the Oedipal norm. Fortunately, this norm has only partially succeeded in imposing itself.

Note

1 A sign represents something for someone. A signifier represents the subject for another signifier. Lacan writes on this issue: "Elle [Anna O.] montre quoi? – on peut spéculer, il faudrait encore ne pas se précipiter sur le langage du corps. Disons simplement que la sexualité montre un fonctionnement naturel des signes. A ce niveau ce ne sont pas des signifiants, car le faux-ballon est un symptôme, et selon la définition du signe, quelque chose pour quelqu'un. Le signifiant, étant tout autre chose, représente un sujet pour un autre significant" (Lacan 1973: 144).

References

Butler, J. (1983). *Bodies that Matter: On the Discursive Limits of "Sex"*. London: Routledge.
David-Ménard, M. (1983). *L'hystérique entre Freud et Lacan*. Paris: Editions Universitaires.
David-Ménard, M. (ed.) (2009). *Sexualités, genres et mélancolie: S'entretenir avec Judith Butler*. Paris: Campagne Première.
David-Ménard, M. (2014). *Corps et langage en psychanalyse: L'hystérique entre Freud et Lacan*. Paris: Campagne Première.
Derrida, J. (1967). Cogito et histoire de la folie. In *L'écriture et la différence*, Paris: Seuil, 51–98.
Descartes, R. (1967 [1641]). *Méditations, Première Méditation, Œuvres philosophiques, tome II*. Paris: Garnier.
Feldman, S. (1922). Über das Erröten. *Internationale Zeitschrift für Psychoanalye* 1, 14 ff.
Foucault, M. (1972). *Histoire de la folie à l'âge classique*. Paris: Gallimard.
Freud, S. (1895). *Studies on Hysteria*. J. Strachey (ed.), *Standard Edition 1*. London: Hogarth.
Freud, S. (1900). *The Interpretation of Dreams, SE 4–5*.
Freud, S. (1905). *Three Essays on the Theory of Sexuality, SE 7*.
Freud, S. (1909). Some General Remarks on Hysterical Attacks, *SE 9*.
Freud, S. (1915). Instincts and their Vicissitudes, *SE 14*.
Freud, S. (1918). From the History of an Infantile Neurosis, *SE 17*.
Freud, S. (1920a). *Beyond the Pleasure Principle, SE 18*.
Freud, S. (1920b). The Psychogenesis of a Case of Homosexuality in a Woman, *SE 18*.
Freud, S. (1925). Negation, *SE 19*.
Freud, S. (1933). New Introductory Lectures on Psycho-Analysis, *SE 22*.
Freud, S. (1950 [1895]). Project for a Scientific Psychology, *SE 1*.

Lacan, J. (1966). *Écrits*. Paris: Seuil.
Lacan, J. (1973). *Le Séminaire Livre XI, Les quartre concepts fandamenteaux de la psychanalyse*. Paris: Seuil.
Landauer, K. (1926). Die kindliche Bewegungsunruhe: Das Schicksal der den Stammganglien unterstehenden triebhaften Bewegungen. *Internationale Zeitschrift für Psychoanalye* 12, 379–390.
Spinoza, B. (1996 [1677]). *Ethics*. London: Penguin.

7

LACAN MEETS FREUD?

Patho-analytic reflections on the status of the perversions in Lacanian Metapsychology

Philippe Van Haute

Introduction

From its inception, psychoanalysis has presented and understood itself as a liberating theory and practice. Freud and his pupils considered psychoanalysis, both in its theoretical and practical aspects, as an enterprise that could free us from all kinds of oppressive cultural norms, particularly with regard to sexuality. Psychoanalysis was thought to be a threat to bourgeois sexual culture. Along the same lines Lacan introduced the apocryphal story that while on their way to the United States in 1909, Freud told Jung that they were bringing the plague to the New World (Roudinesco 2014: 194). Clearly, Lacan also saw psychoanalysis as a revolutionary movement with regard to the psychiatric and cultural establishment. Contemporary psychoanalysts frequently repeat this pretence.

It is hard to deny that Freudian psychoanalysis in many respects had a liberating potential and that psychoanalysis did contribute to profound changes in our cultural and moral landscape. Freud was, for example, one of the first to de-pathologize homosexuality, and his ideas on (infantile) sexuality and on sexual education testify to an attitude that was at odds with the fundamental tendencies of his time. As is well known, the problem of the perversions plays a crucial role in this context. Nineteenth-century psychiatry and sexology considered the sexual perversions exclusively as specific diagnostic entities that fitted certain patients and not others. Perversion was understood as a psychopathology, alongside hysteria, neurasthenia and multiple personality (Davidson 2001a). For Freud, however, the perversions, like the other pathologies that are central to his thought (i.e. hysteria, obsessional neurosis and paranoia), have an anthropological value. According to Freud, the different psychopathological categories inform us about the fundamental tendencies and problematics that constitute human existence as such. This means, more concretely, that with regard to our sexual existence, the perversions show in a magnified way the building blocks that make up the sexuality of every one of us. Freudian psychoanalysis is a patho-analysis (Van Haute & Geyskens 2012). It takes psychopathology as a starting point for its anthropology and in doing so deconstructs the problematic opposition between 'normality' and pathology. According to Davidson, this implies a radical critique of what he calls 'a psychiatric style of reasoning' (Davidson 2001a: 68–69).

Nevertheless, Freud himself would turn away from the liberating potential of his own metapsychology. Indeed, the reference to the Oedipus and castration complex introduced a more normalizing tendency to his theories (Van Haute & Geyskens 2012; Van Haute 2014). This reference contradicts the patho-analytic approach that at the same time remains present in many of Freud's writings. Whatever the case may be, the normalizing tendencies gained the upper hand in many post-Freudian writings and in psychoanalytic practice. They are still dominant in many psychoanalytic quarters today (Tort 2005: 423–434).

Freud (and with him many of his followers) seems to betray the radical and liberating aspects of his own theory. As a result, psychoanalysis risks becoming a normalizing theory.[1] It is impossible to develop this problematic in all of its aspects and in relation to all the different psychoanalytic traditions within the context of just one chapter. Hence, I will limit myself in this chapter to the problem of the status of the so-called perversions in the Freudian-Lacanian tradition.[2] Indeed, the reference to the problem of the perversions plays a foundational role in this tradition. Freud's reflections on the patho-analytic approach to human existence allows for a radical critique of the very idea of the perversions as a legitimate psychopathological category. What is put into question is the very legitimacy of differential diagnosis with regard to the perversions.[3] I will discuss this approach in the first edition of the *Three Essays on the Theory of Sexuality*. This first edition differs on crucial points from the later editions we are familiar with and that were published in the *Standard Edition* and in the *Gesammelte Werke*. It is particularly interesting and important for our discussion because it does not contain some of the normalizing concepts and theories (e.g. the developmental perspective and the Oedipus complex) that were only introduced in the later editions.[4]

My argument is that references to a perverse *structure* that is popular in some Lacanian circles, seem to break with this patho-analytic approach. It re-introduces the very idea of a differential 'identity' that Freud deconstructed. In doing so, its adherents risk falling into all kinds of social and moral prejudices that are subsequently presented as laws that structure sexuality (and society) as such, and that transcend history and the socio-cultural environments in which they occur. In this way, social and moral prejudices tend to be immunized from critique and in the process they acquire an ideological status. I will first discuss the Freudian approach to perversion and then contrast this approach to Lacanian orthodoxy and more particularly the idea of a perverse structure. In my conclusion, I will return to the historical and cultural context that might explain at least partially Lacan's problematic account of the perversions.

The pervert, my neighbour? The genesis of the sexual perversions and the Freudian revolution

We all know the traditional list of perversions that was described in great detail by Krafft-Ebing and other sexologists at the end of the nineteenth century: homosexuality, fetishism, sado-masochism, voyeurism and exhibitionism (Krafft-Ebing 1903). Foucault, Davidson and others have shown in the most convincing way that these perversions are not so much described for the first time in the second half of the nineteenth century, but were instead literally created in that period (Foucault 1976; Davidson 2001a). These authors maintain that there were no perversions (and also no homo- or heterosexuality) before the second half of the nineteenth century. They obviously do not mean that there was no perverse behaviour before this period (or that prior to this people would not have been interested in sex for that matter). They claim, on the contrary, that these acts and activities were only from then on considered to be the expression of a specific type of individual, a specific kind of subjective identity that shows itself, for example, in particular character traits that are the result of a specific psychosexual history and development (Foucault 1976, *passim*; Davidson 2001a, 22 ff). Making reference to Ian Hacking, one could say that it is only from the second half of the nineteenth century onwards that perversion becomes a 'possibility of personhood' (Hacking 2002: 107). Davidson links this possibility to the development of a 'psychiatric style of reasoning' that determines its presuppositions. In this 'style of reasoning', psychological explanations centred around the very notion of personality play an important role (Davidson 2001a: 63). From a historical perspective, the psychiatric style of reasoning replaces an anatomo-pathological style of reasoning. In this latter style, deviant behaviour is consistently linked to anatomical changes or to lesions in the neurological substratum. Hence, for instance, serious attempts were made to link homosexuality to changes in the male organ (Davidson 2001a: 6). It was thought, for instance – the hypothesis turned out to be incorrect – that homosexuals would have a penis in the shape of a corkscrew. There is insufficient place to discuss the whole history of nineteenth-century sexology in all its juicy details, but it is all too clear that it is the absence of organic lesions (for instance, in the case of homosexuality) that forced sexologists and psychiatrists to determine the perversions (but also, for example, hysteria) as functional diseases. Or, more precisely, it is only at the very moment that sexuality is defined as a function which like other functions can be disturbed without there being a specific organic cause or neurological lesion, that the perversions can be described as a separate category or class of phenomena that intrinsically belong together (Davidson 2001a: 74 and *passim*).[5] Only when sexuality is seen as a (reproductive) function – and this is exactly the definition that Krafft-Ebing uses in the beginning of *Psychopathia Sexualis* (1903) – can the different perversions be categorized under one label as the different disorders of this function. Only from this point on does a 'perverse (psychological) identity' that is essentially different from other 'identities' become possible.

All of these developments belong to the context in which Freud articulates his insights on human sexuality and its role in psychopathology. I will limit my discussion of Freud to the first edition of the *Three Essays* (Freud 1905a, 1905b),[6] which is fundamentally different from the later editions that were published in 1910, 1915, 1920 and 1924. In this first edition there is, for instance, no reference to the Oedipus and the castration complexes. In this first version the idea of a progressive psychic development is also almost completely absent. These theories were only introduced in the later editions (Van Haute 2014). It is already clear from this that the first edition of the *Three Essays* differs in many respects from what is often assumed to be characteristic of Freudian theory (Van Haute & Westerink 2015). But one thing does not change in the subsequent editions of the text: Freud's starting point. As is well known, the first part of the text discusses the 'sexual aberrations', that is, the different perversions as they had been defined (mainly) by Krafft-Ebing. It is with these 'aberrations' that Freud begins (Freud 1905a: 1 ff, 1905b: 135 ff). The importance of this gesture should be immediately evident. The sexologists at the end of the nineteenth and beginning of the twentieth century took the supposedly normal (reproductive) functioning of sexuality as their starting point. From there it became possible to define the perversions as deviations of this function. Freud, on the other hand, calls the very idea of sexuality as a reproductive function a 'poetic fable' (Freud 1905a: 2, 1905b: 136), and he literally turns the argumentation of his fellow sexologists upside down; to understand sexuality we should not start from a supposedly 'normal' function, but from what we consider to be 'deviations' of this function. Indeed, according to Freud, these deviations – the classical 'perversions' – show us the constitutive elements of sexuality as such. This means, more concretely, that the different perversions reveal the building blocks of human sexuality in an isolated and magnified way. Sadism confronts us, for instance, with an instinct for mastery that belongs to sexuality as such and that otherwise might pass unnoticed (Freud 1905a: *passim*).

It is hard to overestimate the consequences of this patho-analytic turn. Indeed, Freud connects this insight immediately with the idea that sexuality has no object that is ascribed to it by nature (and, furthermore, that the drives only tend towards pleasure) (Freud 1905a: 10, 1905b: 147–148). The starting point of the sexologists is therefore nothing but a chimera. Bearing in mind what was said before regarding Foucault and Davidson, all of this implies that from the outset Freud rejects the very conditions for the existence of the perversions as a separate identity, a separate 'possibility of personhood'. If sexuality cannot be understood as a natural function, if sexuality can, moreover, only be understood from the perspective of its so-called deviations, then it inevitably becomes impossible to classify a group of people as 'perverts', which, from a psychological point of view, would be to make a fundamental distinction between a group who escape 'perversion' and another who do not. Davidson concludes from this that Freud breaks away from the psychiatric style of reasoning as it was defined earlier in this chapter (Davidson 2001a: 71).

The different perversions inform us about the different building blocks of sexuality. What Freud learns from them is that sexuality is constructed out of partial drives (oral, anal . . .) that find their locus in the corresponding erogenous zones. These partial drives only pursue pleasure and are fundamentally autoerotic – this means that they do not aim at an object or, more precisely, that their relation to any and every object has no essential meaning. It is exclusively the capacity of the object to provide pleasure that is at stake here (Freud 1905a: 37, 1905b: 181). The different erogenous zones – and this is absolutely crucial – are not situated in a chronological (or teleological) sequence. There is one passage in the 1905 edition of the *Three Essays* that seems to contradict this idea. This is where Freud writes with respect to infantile genital masturbation, from which hardly anyone escapes, that it is in line with 'nature's purpose' (*die Absicht der Natur*) to prepare the genital zone for the determining role it will have to play in later life (Freud 1905a: 42). When confronted in 1912 by a member of the famous Wednesday evening meetings with the fact that this would introduce a teleological motive to his texts and that nothing prepared for such a motive, Freud immediately gave in and changed his text accordingly (Freud 1905b: 188). From the edition of 1915 onwards, the reference to 'nature's purpose' is left out.[7] Sexuality has no natural object and, even more radically, there cannot be a primacy of the genital zone that is grounded in the nature of sexuality either. Freud is much more radical than many of our contemporary psychoanalysts; he not only maintains that we all have perverse fantasies[8] but also, and this is more fundamental, he deconstructs the essential presuppositions that would allow us to identify a separate category of so-called 'sexual perverts'.

This is what Freud says in 1905. Or, rather, this is what Freud says in the first two chapters of the 1905 edition of the *Three Essays*.[9] In the third chapter entitled 'Transformations of Puberty' Freud seems to defend a completely different position. Here, for instance, Freud writes the following:

> Writers on the subject . . . have asserted that the necessary precondition of a whole number of perverse fixations lies in an innate weakness of the sexual instinct. In this form the view seems to me untenable. It makes sense, however, if what is meant is a constitutional weakness of one particular factor in the sexual instinct, namely the genital zone – a zone which takes over the function of combining the separate sexual activities for the purposes of reproduction. For if the genital zone is weak, this combination, which is required to take place in puberty, is bound to fail, and the strongest of other components of sexuality will continue its activity as a perversion.
>
> (Freud 1905a: 75, 1905b: 237)

How can we reconcile this statement with what Freud has already claimed in the first two chapters of the book under consideration? From a historical point of view it is patently obvious that the sexologists to whom Freud is referring said exactly the same thing as what Freud himself is proposing, namely, that perversion must be linked to a weakness of the genital zone (Davidson 2001a: 89). But this quotation implies a teleological and functional view of sexuality, which was precisely the view that Freud sought to reject in the first two chapters of the book.

Davidson is therefore quite justified in stating that in light of his own argumentation, Freud could only have said the following:

> For if the genital zone is weak, this combination which often takes place at puberty (instead of: 'which is *required* to take place in puberty' . . . this indeed implies a functional/teleological interpretation, PvH), will fail, and the strongest of the other components of sexuality will continue its activity (instead of: 'will continue its activity *as a perversion*' . . . the latter implies that there exists a 'pervert identity' that can be described as such, PvH).
> (Davidson 2001a: 89)

The perverse structure

Let us now turn to Lacan and his followers in order to consider the way in which they rethink the status of the sexual perversions. My aim here is neither to analyse the totality of Lacan's texts nor to give a detailed account of everything Lacan wrote on the perversions, which, in fact, was not that much. Rather I will limit myself to the idea of a perverse *structure*, which is very popular in many Lacanian circles and which is supposed to be essentially different from the neurotic and psychotic structures (Fink 1997; Verhaeghe 2001, 2004; Swales 2012; Bonny & Maleval 2015). According to Verhaeghe, the theory of the different structures of the subject is generally accepted in contemporary Lacanian theory (Verhaeghe 2001: 77). While this idea is undoubtedly based on some of Lacan's most fundamental assumptions,[10] it would nevertheless be unjust to reduce his thinking on this topic to the idea that perversion, or the perverse structure as it is often called, is essentially different from the other two structures just mentioned. Lacan cannot be reduced to the textbook versions of his thinking. Hence, in his famous text 'Kant with Sade' Lacan tries to understand the basic characteristics of human desire *as such* from the perspective of sadism and, more particularly, the work of Sade himself (Lacan 1966). Lacan here defends a patho-analytic approach that makes it impossible to reduce 'sadism' to a specific perversion next to other perversions. Sadism is in this text not exclusively interpreted 'next and in opposition to' the other positions. Quite on the contrary, the work of Sade shows, according to Lacan, the impasses of Kant's philosophy and in doing so it allows for the discovery of some fundamental aspects of human desire. There is no place here to give a detailed reading of this difficult text, but it is clear that in it Lacan seems to follow a patho-analytic approach. This approach characterizes, as we already know, Freud's early texts and it goes against the idea of pathological 'identities' that are essentially different from other pathological 'identities'. Lacan's thinking on (the status of) the different structures is, in other words, much less univocal than is sometimes suggested.

But what does this theory of the subjective structures about which there seems to be a general agreement entail? In order to get a clearer idea of this theory, it is worthwhile focusing a little more on Verhaeghe and the way in which he thematizes the perversions in his well-known book on differential diagnosis in psychoanalysis (Verhaeghe 2004). Indeed, Verhaeghe's account of the perversions makes explicit a paradigm that could be said to underlie a number of other Lacanian publications on the same topic (Dor 1987; Miller 1996; Fink 1997; Feher 2003; Lebrun 2007). Like these other authors, Verhaeghe refers in his introduction to the chapter on the perversions in Freud's *Three Essays*. He mentions Freud's insight that human sexuality is essentially polymorph perverse and that the predisposition to perversion is present in all of us. He then concludes as follows: 'Consequently, according to Freudian theory, the distinction between perverse traits and the perverse structure is not easy to make' (Verhaeghe 2004: 403). It is immediately clear that this citation contradicts Freud's patho-analytic perspective that I explained earlier in this chapter. This citation can indeed be rendered as follows: 'Of course, we all have more or less perverse tendencies, and perverse fantasies are quite common . . . but these are irrelevant with regard to an essentially neurotic, psychotic or perverse structure; the real "perversion" is situated elsewhere'. It is worth recalling that the distinction between perverse traits and perversion proper in some ways resonates with a similar distinction that can be found in the work of Krafft-Ebing and other psychiatrists of the nineteenth century. Krafft-Ebing calls perverse transgressions in the context of non-sexual pathologies 'perversities' in otherwise 'healthy' people (*Perversitäten*). The latter are vices that have to be judged from a moral or a juridical point of view. *Perversitäten* are licentious acts committed by people who could do otherwise, but who prefer forbidden pleasures to that which the law considers to be 'normal' or 'good'. As a point of principle, these 'perverse acts' are judged immoral and they often warrant punishment. They have to be strictly distinguished from perversion (*Perversion*) as a disease that 'overrules' the free will and that concerns the whole personality – hence from perversion as a 'possibility of personhood'.[11] It is worth noting that just like contemporary Lacanian authors, Krafft-Ebing considers 'perversion' not only as a distinct type of identity, but as an incurable one at that. Once a pervert, always a pervert!

Rather than reaching a conclusion too hastily, it is worthwhile asking what characterizes the perverse structure according to the authors under consideration. Essentially, Lacan and his followers link perversion to a specific type of relation to (the Other of) the law.[12] Perversion is fundamentally identified with a specific relation to the law of language that introduces lack (or as Lacan puts it: castration) and in doing so makes desire possible. This law is also the law of the father that forbids the mother to take the child as an object that might allow her to overcome her own lack in enjoyment (*jouissance*). Hence, it comes as no surprise that one seeks the origin of the perverse structure in the relation to the first Other – in principle the mother. The perverse subject, so we are indeed told, is stuck in a relation with the first Other in which he is reduced to a phallic object thereby (fantasmatically) allowing her to overcome her lack. In other words, the child is here nothing but the imaginary phallus of the Other (Lacan 1977: 197–198). The father (that is, the law that he represents) is at the same time reduced to a spectator without any power or importance. Hence, castration is both denied (in the mother who is supposed to be able to overcome lack in the relation with her child) and recognized (in the powerless father). Lacan here generalizes the defence mechanism that according to Freud characterizes fetishism in such a way that it now applies to all the perversions. This defence mechanism is *disavowal* (Freud 1927). This mechanism implies that the subject takes a double stance: it both acknowledges and denies castration (Verhaeghe 2004: 411).

This situation confronts the child with a paradox which is, according to our authors, at the basis of the perverse structure and explains its logic. The little child is on the one hand the object that makes the enjoyment of the Other possible, but on the other hand this state of affairs excludes the development of a separate identity. Indeed, as long as the 'infans' remains nothing but the object that fills the lack of the Other, it cannot develop a desire of its own. The child tries to overcome this paradoxical situation by turning itself – actively – into the instrument of the enjoyment of the Other. He is at the service of the enjoyment of the Other, in the possibility of which he continues to firmly believe. The enjoyment of the Other is the goal of all his hard work. This would explain, for instance, why perverse subjects so often claim that the victims of their acts 'also enjoy it' or 'asked for it themselves' (Verhaeghe 2004: 425). The perverse subject, so much is clear, identifies with the object that allows him to overcome lack once and for all. This also implies that the perverse subject does not accept the law of castration and lack. But the enjoyment of the Other would inevitably imply his own disappearance as a desiring subject. There is no desiring subject outside of lack and castration. Hence, the possibility of the enjoyment of the Other provokes anxiety. This anxiety forces the subject to limit enjoyment and hence to introduce a law after all (the masochist, for instance, submits himself to the Other and turns himself into the object of his enjoyment, but at the same time he makes sure not to lose control of the situation and sets a limit).[13] But this law can only be the law of the perverse subject itself, since it belongs to the very structure of perversion to challenge the law of the Other (of the father, who introduces castration). The consequences of this challenge are that the Other is either reduced to a powerless spectator or systematically ridiculed. One can think here of the writings of Sade who 'teaches' the passive Other (those who read his books) about what 'real enjoyment' is and how it radically differs from our petty ('neurotic') pleasures. One sees the difference between the perverse and the neurotic position. In the latter case, castration is acknowledged and the child accepts that neither he nor the father can satisfy the desire of the mother. Here the central question with regard to sexuality becomes: Am I doing well? We are far away here from Sade's writings (Verhaege 2004: 436).

While hardly complete, this description must suffice to indicate what is at stake here. In the first place, Lacan is no longer concerned with the types of sexual behaviour (fetishistic, sadist . . .) that can be linked to a specific identity. These types of behaviour can occur in every structure. Lacan is, on the contrary, much more interested in a structural relation to the law (of the Other). This is what the idea of a perverse structure is about. The notion of a perverse *structure* implies that this relation characterizes a specific group of people in a consistent and invariable way.

Hence, we are talking of a kind of identity or psychological profile (the 'pervert') that no longer threatens human sexuality, but human society as such (Dean 2008). The law that the pervert refuses (the law of the father, of castration . . . sexual difference) is indeed supposed to be the law that founds human society. This law ('no') of the father (that separates us from the first Other) inherently refers to the interdiction of incest or to the obligation of exogamy (and hence to the law of sexual difference) that, according to Lacan, founds human society. As a consequence, the perverse subject does not question this or that *specific* law. On the contrary, it actively subverts the order of legality as such.[14] This probably explains, second, why the qualification 'pervert' is consistently and enthusiastically applied outside the strictly sexual sphere, while the classical *sexual* perversions at the same time (usually with the exception of homosexuality[15]) continue to be used as the paradigms of perversion. Indeed, the law that the perverse subject refuses (or denies) is in the last instance structurally linked to (the law of) *sexual* difference (Feher 2003).[16] In this way, the classical sexual perversions continue to play a pivotal role in the context I am discussing here. Third, these perversions are – just as in the past – both implicitly and explicitly qualified in a negative way. We find this negative qualification both in the clinical context and in theoretical writings. Verhaeghe, for instance, writes that the perversions are close to psychopathy, and he describes perverse subjects as 'potential perpetrators'.[17] Verhaeghe indeed writes that we find a generalized clinical picture of the perverse structure in forensic practice (Verhaeghe 2004: 405 ff).[18] This should not come as a surprise given that perversion is defined in the first place in terms of a defying relation to the law.

This negative attitude towards 'the pervert' runs through the work of other Lacanian authors who appear to exhibit no sympathy whatsoever for the *kind of people* they call 'perverts'. Thus, for instance, Feher writes that nobody 'in his right mind' would call himself 'a pervert' (Feher 2004: 191). She not only claims that nobody sympathizes with perverts, but that 'the strange world of perverse logic' (2004: 205) should only be mistrusted and that queer theory, which is its cultural representative, should therefore be rejected (2004: 203–204).[19] This negative attitude hardly comes as a surprise when we realize that the perversions were first defined as a direct threat to the very existence of human society. Insofar as the traditional perversions continue to have a paradigmatic value within the so-called perverse structure, their negative qualification (and the rejection that this implies) remains intact (or is re-instated[20]). We are confronted here with an ambiguity that is hard to resolve: on the one hand the problem of perversion cannot be limited to that of the 'sexual aberrations', while on the other, the latter continues to be its most preferred paradigm. In this way, the classical sexual perversions continue to participate in the negative reputation that accompanies perversions and that Freud (but also Krafft-Ebing) wanted to overcome.[21] We are far removed here from Freud's initial intuitions.

I suggested earlier that Lacanian theorists tend to reintroduce the idea of a 'perverse identity'. In doing so I obviously wanted to indicate that the way in which these theorists thematize 'subjective positions' might signal a regressive shift back to the psychiatric style of reasoning that Freud, at least initially, rejected for the reasons already outlined. One could of course object that nineteenth-century sexology took its starting point in an allegedly 'normal' sexual function and that Lacan and the Lacanians of whom I speak do not accept a 'normal' position or structure next to a perverse or neurotic one. But things might be more complicated than they seem. The three structures that are distinguished in Lacanian theory are evidently not at the same level. Put in a brutal way, we could say that there exists a neurotic next to a psychotic position and then there are 'potential perpetrators'. The perverse structure is time and again evaluated in a negative way in relation to the two other structures. But that is not all – at the same time, the neurotic position or structure tends to be described as the 'normal' one. There are many examples that illustrate this tendency. Verhaeghe speaks of a 'normal-neurotic context' (Verhaeghe 2004: 418), and he further calls the psychoanalyst 'normal-neurotic' (2004: 439). In this way, Verhaeghe implicitly turns the neurotic structure or position into the standard for a 'better way of living'. Along similar lines, Fink writes of a perverse patient that there is 'little hope' (sic!) that he will ever become neurotic. Citing Freud's essay 'The Splitting of the Ego' (Freud 1940), the same author adds the term 'neurotic' between brackets after 'normal' to a quote where Freud speaks of the 'normal consequences of castration anxiety' (Fink 1997: 197). Thus, despite appearances, these Lacanian authors – in a much more systematic way then Lacan himself – clearly betray Freudian patho-analysis. Perversion no longer informs us about sexuality as such, but is reduced to a particular (pathological) structure next to other structures. This specific structure does not in principle have anything to teach us about human desire as such.

The influence of French psychiatry: Dupré?

The Lacanian perversion – the idea of a 'perverse structure' – seems to participate in a universe that is not exactly the same as the one that determines Freud's ideas on perversion. We are used to thinking of Lacan and Lacanian theory in terms of a 'return to Freud'. But can we properly understand this theory – especially with regard to the perversions – without taking the French psychiatric tradition into account, in which Lacan was educated as a psychiatrist? Or, more concretely: is not Lacan with regard to the perversions a pupil of Ernest Dupré rather then a pupil of Krafft-Ebing (and consequently of Freud)? Dupré influenced in a hegemonic fashion French psychiatry with regard to the problem of the perversions until at least 1960 (Lantéri-Laura 2012: 129–137; Mazaleigue 2014). Dupré belongs to the generation of de Clérambault – whom Lacan called his 'master in psychiatry' – and whose influence on Lacanian thinking also remains insufficiently studied. As I do not have enough place here to give a detailed account of the relation between Lacan (the idea of a perverse structure) and Dupré, I will limit myself to formulating the outlines of a hypothesis.

In spite of the important differences that separate Lacan and Dupré, there are some troubling similarities that deserve our attention. It is true that Dupré desexualizes the perversions even more then Lacan does. In his work, the sexual perversions no longer function as a paradigm of perversion in general. They are nothing but one species among others (perversions of the instinct of conservation and of the instinct of association) (Dupré 1925: 367 et *passim*). Dupré furthermore postulates an innate perverse constitution that in the end is nothing other than a tendency to inflict harm and do wrong (or to prefer what is bad over what is good) (Dupré 1925: 419; Lantéri-Laura 2012: 133). Obviously a (perverse) structure cannot be identified with a constitution in the biologist sense of the word as in the work of Dupré. But one can wonder whether the former is not its reversed mirror image. Of course, the perverse structure is not innate in the same way as Dupré's biological constitution is. But its genesis goes so far back, that it tends to transcend historical time (Lantéri-Laura 2012: 167). This explains its immutable and undeclinable (uncurable) character that it shares with a biological constitution. On top of that, the perverse structure is explicitly linked – as is the perverse constitution, although for different reasons – to psychopathia and hence to the problem of evil. It follows from this that the perverse structure essentially transcends sexuality, even if at the same time it cannot be understood as separate from it in Lacan, for the reasons I explained before. Although this hypothesis is still tentative, Lantéri-Laura's conclusion certainly no longer comes as a surprise: 'the notion of a perverse structure ... (assures), 40 years after Dupré, exactly the same role as that of constitution, and also in order to re-install a neo-moralism' (Lantéri-Laura 2012: 185, my translation).[22]

Conclusion

The Freudian deconstruction of 'normality' turned perversion into a universal human condition. Specifically, it made it impossible to present perversion as a separate (psychological) identity. From a Freudian perspective, one could say that since everybody is 'perverse', nobody can be a pervert in the sense of an identity that is essentially different from other identities. The perverse subject, in other words, is not just an 'Other' with whom I have nothing in common. Of course, this does not mean that for Freud *in sexualibus* 'anything goes'. On the contrary, Freud links the different partial drives in his *Three Essays* to reaction formations – basically shame and disgust (but he also mentions guilt, for example) – that put limits on our innate perverse tendencies (Freud 1905a: 35, 1905b: 151 ff). These reaction formations are the starting point for the development of cultural prohibitions and obligations with regard to sexuality. Hence, for Freud, there is no sexuality without limits and without conflict. But the laws we make with regard to it cannot, without great difficulty, be linked to a supposed 'nature' of sexuality. They are essentially historical and contingent and hence subject to criticism and debate (Van Haute & Westerink 2015).

From this Freudian point of view, thinking in terms of psychopathological positions threatens to be inevitably anachronistic. Perversions become once again identities – indeed, identities of a despicable nature – that are essentially different from other 'identities'. The fact that the (universal) 'perverse traits' are no longer rejected as morally bad and inadmissible is no real consolation, since it is now the pathological state itself that is systematically judged in a negative way or that tends to be qualified as intrinsically 'bad' or 'evil'. This is at least paradoxical. The history of nineteenth-century psychiatry and sexology can in a certain way be summarized as a permanent (and largely unsuccessful?[23]) attempt to separate psychiatric scientific thinking from moral and religious prejudices on the basis of which we consider all kinds of sexual practices to be 'bad' or 'morally wrong'. This is precisely the reason why Kraft-Ebbing, for instance, separates 'perversities' that are morally reprehensible from 'perversions' that are mental illnesses. Freud still goes one step further by 'deconstructing' the very idea of 'perversion' as a separate identity and by turning it into a universal human disposition. In the Lacanian tradition, these two aspects risk becoming conflated once again.[24] What characterizes the perversions is precisely a structurally twisted and defiant relation to the law that founds human society. And once perversion is characterized as the systematic undermining of the laws of society as such, one should not find it too surprising that the perversions quite often evoke a (violent) moral rejection. This rejection seems to repeat in many respects the presuppositions and prejudices of traditional French psychiatry that Lacan knew from his psychiatric training.

However, we cannot understand this regressive movement by simply referring to the historical background of Lacanian thinking. There are in my opinion at least two more elements that need mentioning here. First of all – and despite appearances – the Lacanian authors under discussion reject the patho-analytic perspective that I have argued is intrinsically linked to a deconstruction of perverse identity. A second reason might be even more interesting, at least from a philosophical point of view. Partly as a consequence of Lacan's work, it has become customary to think about sexuality from the perspective of sexual difference. But is it possible to think of sexuality in this way without being at the same time (and for the same reason) hetero-normative? This would mean disqualifying or subordinating 'positions' in which sexual difference is denied to positions in which it is supposed not to be. In the first edition of the *Three Essays*, Freud does not thematize sexuality from the perspective of sexual difference so much as from the perspective of non-functional bodily pleasures.[25] The perversions are thought to be strange ways of procuring oneself bodily pleasures, but there is no intrinsic principle that allows one to subordinate one form of pleasure to another form of pleasure. In Lacan, on the contrary, what characterizes the perverse subject is not so much the bodily pleasures the subject is looking for, but the twisted and transgressive way in which the subject relates to the law.[26] Lacan does not define perverse enjoyment in terms of bodily pleasures but, for instance, in terms of the anxiety it provokes in the Other (Lacan 2004).

It is the thematization of sexuality in terms of bodily pleasures, together with the patho-analytic perspective that makes a deconstruction of perversion as a separate identity both possible and necessary. In this way, my journey through the problematic of the perversions ends (at least provisionally) where it started: with Foucault. Indeed, it does not require too much imagination to discover Foucault's *corps des plaisirs* in Freud's sexual pleasures (Davidson 2001b). Perhaps for the moment we should therefore conclude that if psychoanalysis is to remain true to Freud's most important insights, then it will be a Foucauldian enterprise.

Notes

1 In more recent times, Jean Laplanche has no doubt been very attentive to this thematic (see e.g. Laplanche 2007). His theory of a generalized seduction implies a ferocious critique of the developmental approach to psychoanalysis, the Oedipus complex and Lacan's primacy of the phallus. In this way, Laplanche tries to free psychoanalysis from its normalizing tendencies (Van Haute & Geyskins 2004; Laplanche 2007).
2 In what follows I will not discuss the relation between homosexuality and psychoanalysis. This relation is and remains in many ways very ambiguous and complicated (Dean & Lane 2001). It is all too obvious that many psychoanalysts still defend highly problematic positions on the topic. The recent debates in France among psychoanalysts on same sex marriage, for example, testifies to this extremely conservative attitude. Analysing the different positions and ideas on this issue would lead us too far astray. For an overview, see Roudinesco (2002).
3 And more generally this also concerns differential diagnosis as such. When psychopathology informs us about who we are and shows the fundamental tendencies and problematics that are operative in all of us, it becomes very difficult to think of the different pathologies as independent 'identities' that can be clearly distinguished from one another, let alone from an alleged 'normality'.
4 This first edition is in fact hard to find. There is no English translation of it available at present. An English translation of the 1905 edition is currently in preparation by Ulrike Kirstner, Herman Westerink and myself for publication with Verso in 2016. For a recent German edition, see S. Freud, *Drei Abhandlungen zur Sexualtheorie*, P. Van Haute, C. Huber & H. Westerink (eds), Vienna, Austria: Vienna University Press, 2015.
5 For a critical assessment of this historical account of sexuality and perversion, see Mazaleigue (2014).
6 I will only thematize the first edition. I will quote from both the German 1905 (1905a) edition and the 1924 (1905b) edition that one finds in the *Standard Edition*.
7 Starting with the 1915 edition, the passage reads as follows: 'It is scarcely possible to avoid the conclusion that the foundations for the future primacy over sexual activity exercised by this erotogenic zone are established by early infantile masturbation, which scarcely a single individual escapes' (Freud 1905b: 188).
8 One finds this interpretation of Freud's theories in texts of the most well-informed and intelligent psychoanalysts. See e.g. Florence (2005).
9 The introduction of a developmental approach together with the introduction of the Oedipus complex in later versions fundamentally changes Freud's perspective and introduces a normalizing approach. It is beyond the scope of this chapter to develop an account of these changes. For a more detailed account see Van Haute (2014) and Van Haute & Westerink (2015).
10 'The whole problem of the perversions consists in conceiving how the child in relation to the mother, a relation constituted in analysis not by his vital dependence on her, but by his dependence on her love, that is to say, by the desire of her desire, identifies himself with the imaginary object of this desire in as far as the mother herself symbolizes it in the fallus' (Lacan 1977: 197–198).
11 'Perversion of the sexual instinct ... is not to be confounded with perversity in the sexual act; since the latter may be induced by conditions other than psychopathological. The concrete perverse act, monstrous as it may be, is clinically not decisive. In order to differentiate between disease (perversion) and vice (perversity), one must investigate the whole personality of the individual and the original motive leading to the perverse act. Therein will be found the key to the diagnosis' (Krafft-Ebing 1965: 53).

12 For what follows, see e.g. Verhaeghe (2004: 397–427); Swales (2012).
13 This is why Lacan calls the perversion a *père-version*.
14 Stephanie Swales writes in this respect: 'The perverse subject is he who has undergone alienation but disavowed castration, suffering from excessive jouissance and a core belief that the law and social norms are fraudulent at worse and weak at best' (Swales 2012: xii).
15 The attitude of many Lacanian psychoanalysts with regard to homosexuality remains quite ambiguous. For a more detailed account of this problematic, see Roudinesco (2002) and Tort (2005).
16 Indeed, the pervert presents himself as the object that can fulfil the lack of the Other and in doing so denies sexual difference. He is a 'homosexual' (Lacan 1973: 78).
17 'The fine line between victim and perpetrator is often transgressed …'. (Verhaeghe 2004: 429).
18 For example, Verhaeghe writes: 'In the conventional world, the law will apparently be followed, that is to say the pervert acts on the assumption that others will follow the conventional rules and he or she will make full use of this knowledge' (Verhaeghe 2004: 412). In a footnote to this passage he adds: 'The association with the old psychopathy is quite clear'.
19 Judith Feher clearly has no idea about what 'informal fallacies' are …
20 We should indeed remember that classical sexology tried to get rid of these negative qualifications by claiming that the perversions were mental diseases and escaped our free will. The consequence of this is that pervert subjects deserve our help and attention, not rejection.
21 Stephanie Swales whom I already quoted before (see note 14) is a perfect example of this. On the one hand, she defines the perverse subject as somebody for whom the law is fraudulent, while at the same time – and under the same 'heading' giving a very detailed account of the different sexual perversions (Swales 2012).
22 'La notion de structure perverse … (assure), quarante ans après E. Dupré, exactement le même office que celle de constitution, et aussi pour restituer un néo-moralisme'.
23 Lacan's theory of the perversions should in this respect be re-contextualized from the perspective of the history of psychiatric thinking on the topic. For more on this problem, see Mazaleigue (2014: 290).
24 'Perverse traits' that occur in neurotic and psychotic structures are no longer seen as intrinsically problematic or morally 'wrong' as in Krafft-Ebing. It may not be unfair to say that for the Lacanian authors under consideration they are nothing but 'sexual frivolities' that do not deserve further attention.
25 For a discussion of this problem, see Butler (1999).
26 The idea that the perverse enjoyment is intrinsically linked to provoking anxiety in the Other (Lacan 2004) illustrates the same problematic. See also, Mazaleigue (2014: 290).

References

Bonny, P. & Maleval, J.-C. (2015). Evolution du concept de structure perverse-fétichiste dans le courant lacanien: La théorie et sa clinique. *Evolution psychiatrique*, http://www.sciencedirect.com/science/article/pii/S0014385515000900 (accessed 16 November 2015).
Butler, J. (1999). Revisiting Bodies & Pleasures. *Theory, Culture and Society* 16(2), 11–20.
Davidson, A. (2001a). *The Emergence of Sexuality: Historical Epistemology and the Formation of Concepts*. Cambridge, MA: Harvard University Press.
Davidson, A. (2001b). Foucault, Psychoanalysis and Pleasure. In T. Dean & C. Lane (eds.), *Homosexuality and Psychoanalysis* (pp. 43–50). Chicago, IL: University of Chicago Press.
Dean, T. (2008). The Frozen Countenance of Perversions. *Parallax* 14:2, 93–114.
Dean, T. & Lane, C. (2001). *Homosexuality and Psychoanalysis*. Chicago, IL: University of Chicago Press.
Dor, J. (1987). *Structure et perversion*. Paris: Denoël.

Dupré, E. (1925). *Les perversions instinctives, dans Pathologie de l'imagination et de l'émotivité.* Paris: Payot.
Feher, J. (2003). A Lacanian Approach to the Problem of Perversion. In J.-M. Rabaté (ed.), *The Cambridge Companion to Lacan.* Cambridge, MA: Cambridge University Press, 191–207.
Fink, B. (1997). *Clinical Introduction to Lacanian Psychoanalysis: Theory and Technique.* Cambridge, MA: Harvard University Press.
Florence, J. (2005). Du désir et de la perversion ordinaire. *Cahiers de psychologie clinique* 24:1, 49–62.
Foucault, M. (1976). *Histoire de la sexualité 1: La volonté de savoir.* Paris: Seuil.
Freud, S. (1905a). *Drei Abhandlungen zur Sexualtheorie.* Leipzig and Vienna: Deuticke.
Freud, S. (1905b). *Three Essays on the Theory of Sexuality.* J. Strachey (ed.), *Standard Edition 7.* London: Hogarth.
Freud, S. (1927). Fetishism, *SE 21.*
Freud, S. (1940). The Splitting of the Ego, *SE 20.*
Hacking, I. (2002). Making up People. In *Historical Ontology.* Cambridge, MA: Harvard University Press, 99–114.
Krafft-Ebing, R. von (1903). *Psychopathia Sexualis, With Especial Reference to the Antipathic Sexual Instinct: A Medico-Forensic Study.* Transl. F.E. Klaf, New York: Arcade, 1965.
Lacan, J. (1966). *Écrits.* Paris: Seuil.
Lacan, J. (1973). *Encore: Le séminaire de Jacques Lacan.* J.-A. Miller (ed.). Paris: Seuil.
Lacan, J. (1977). *Ecrits: A Selection.* New York and London: Norton Company.
Lacan, J. (2004). *L'angoisse: Le séminaire de Jacques Lacan.* J.-A. Miller (ed.). Paris: Seuil.
Lantéri-Laura, G. (2012). *Lecture des perversions: Histoire de leur appropriation medical.* Paris: Economica/Anthropos.
Laplanche, J. (2007). *Sexual: La sexualité élargie au sens de Freud.* Paris: PUF (Quadrige).
Lebrun, J.-P. (2007). *La perversion originaire.* Paris: Payot.
Mazaleigue, J. (2014). *Les déséquilibres de l'amour: La genèse du concept de perversion sexuelle, de la revolution française à Freud.* Paris: Ithaque.
Miller, J.-A. (1996). On Perversion. In R. Feldstein, B. Fink & M. Jaanus (eds.), *Reading Seminars I and II: Lacan's Return to Freud.* Albany, NY: State University of New York Press, 306–320.
Roudinesco, E. (2002). Psychanalyse et homosexualité: reflexions sur le désir pervers, l'injure et la function paternelle. *Cliniques méditérannéennes* 65, 7–35.
Roudinesco, E. (2014). *Sigmund Freud en son temps et dans le nôtre.* Paris: Seuil.
Swales, S. (2012). *Perversion: A Lacanian Psychoanalytic Approach to the Subject.* New York: Routledge.
Tort, M. (2005). *Fin du dogme paternal.* Paris: Aubier.
Van Haute, P. (2014). Freud against Oedipus. *Radical Philosophy* 188, 39–46.
Van Haute P. & Geyskens, T. (2004). *Confusion of Tongues: The Primacy of Sexuality in Freud, Ferenczi and Laplanche.* New York: Other Press.
Van Haute, P. & Geyskens, T. (2012). *A Non-Oedipal Psychoanalysis? A Clinical Anthropology of Hysteria in the Work of Freud and Lacan.* Leuven: Leuven University Press.
Van Haute, P. & Westerink, H. (2015). Hysterie, Sexualität und Psychiatrie: Eine Relektüre der ersten Ausgabe der *Drei Abhandlungen zur Sexualtheorie.* In S. Freud, *Drei Abhandlungen zur Sexualtheorie (1905),* C. Huber, P. Van Haute & H. Westerink (eds.). Vienna, Austria: Vienna University Press, 9–56.
Verhaeghe, P. (2001). Perversion II: The Perverse Structure. *The Letter* 23, 77–95.
Verhaeghe, P. (2004). *On Being Normal and Other Disorders: A Manual for Clinical Diagnostics.* New York: Other Press.

EPILOGUE

The Three Essays *today*

Philippe Van Haute and
Herman Westerink

Freud's *Three Essays* marks the end of an era. In this book the great sexological tradition of Krafft-Ebing and his contemporaries meets the psychiatric reflection on hysteria. Soon after the publication of the *Three Essays* in 1905 classical ('Charcotian') hysteria started to disappear from the psychiatric agenda (Micale 1993). Many of the symptoms that had characterized it were from now on linked to new diagnostic categories such as schizophrenia, and thanks to new medical techniques such as the electro-encephalogram, hysteria itself could be better distinguished from epilepsy. It is impossible to understand Freud's foundational text without a thorough examination and reconstruction of this historical context. Without such a reconstruction we will never grasp, for instance, why after 1905 Freud turns his attention away from hysteria towards obsessional neurosis and psychosis as new paradigms for the understanding of pathology and human existence in general. The evolution of Freudian thinking cannot be understood on the basis of internal motives alone. This evolution is also determined by external elements – particularly in the history of psychiatry – that need to be evaluated.

This interaction between internal and external elements is crucial for understanding the relation between the different editions of the *Three Essays*. In the first edition, Freud makes a sharp distinction between two regimes of sexual pleasure: autoerotic pleasure that characterizes infantile sexuality and adult sexuality that sets in at the beginning of puberty. Adult sexual pleasure is essentially object-related. As long as Freud used hysteria as the model for the understanding of pathology and human existence, the finding of the object did not become a special problem. Indeed, in hysteria the constitution and the existence of the object are never really put into question. But once hysteria disappeared from the psychiatric agenda, Freud turned his attention to the pathologies that replaced hysteria, and more particularly to psychosis. Jung had already written a whole chapter on the similarities between hysteria and dementia praecox, which was soon to be renamed schizophrenia (Jung 1907: 81–115). Freud's interest in psychosis – and in turning psychoanalysis into a paradigm for psychiatry – meant that he was confronted with the fact that (the relation with) the object can be absent or profoundly disturbed. In the same period, he 'accidently discovers' the importance of infantile object choice in his case study of Little Hans' phobia, and in particular in the boy's sexual curiosity and philosophy of life. Hence, he had to deal with the problem of the constitution of the object in the years following the first edition of the *Three Essays*. In line with his patho-analyic approach, Freud found an answer to this problem in psychosis (the introduction of narcissism as a first relation to the object) and in obsessional neurosis (the Oedipus complex as a nuclear moment in the psychic development of each individual). From the third edition that appeared in 1915 onward, the developmental approach will take the lead. One sees how this evolution is determined by both internal problems and the changing historical context.

But the *Three Essays* does not simply bring an era to a close, the text also opens up new theoretical possibilities. In this text Freud can also be seen to break with the 'psychiatric style of reasoning' (Davidson 2001). This 'style of reasoning' operates with categorical terms and posits as a result a strict distinction between normality and pathology. In his *Three Essays* Freud opposes the patho-analytic approach to this 'style of reasoning'. Humans can only be understood from the perspective of the different psychopathologies of which they are capable. These pathologies show, in a magnified way, the tendencies and problematics that structure the existence of the human being. As a result, the psychiatric (nosological) categories receive an anthropological value. They no longer refer to specific 'identities' that fit certain people and not others, but reveal the fundamental tendencies that are present in all of us and characterize our existence. With regard to sexuality, this methodological idea implies that we cannot but give up the distinction between perverse and normal sexuality. When the presumably pathological forms of sexuality ('*Die sexuelle Abirrungen*') lay bare the building blocks of human sexuality and when, furthermore, the system of these tendencies or (partial) drives is fundamentally governed by the search for pleasure (and the avoidance of unpleasure), how then can we maintain a strict distinction between what is pathological ('perverse') and what is not? There is indeed no intrinsic criterion that would allow us to differentiate between different kinds of pleasure. Hence the pathologization of certain types of sexual behaviour has, according to Freud, an essentially historical and social character that needs to be examined.

Nevertheless, Freud is not always very consistent when it comes to his overall approach. Already in the first edition of his *Three Essays* he claims both that the idea of an innate heterosexual instinct is a 'poetic fable' and that heterosexual relations are the natural outcome of the psychosexual development in the individual. This ambiguity increases in later editions where Freud explicates and systematically elaborates a developmental approach and, above all, introduces the Oedipus complex. Freud is clearly struggling in the different editions of this text, as he is in the rest of his work, with the radical consequences of his own thinking. To renounce the distinction between pathology and normality in general and between pathological and healthy forms of sexuality in particular was, even for Freud, far from clear-cut.

The paradoxes that characterize the different editions of the *Three Essays* determine to a large extent the history of the psychoanalytic debates on sexuality. Authors that (consciously or not) are mainly inspired by the first edition of this text (or by passages from it) are more inclined to defend very liberal positions. They think that the different sexual orientations that we know are merely variations without any pathological significance. Indeed, in the first edition of the *Three Essays* Freud discusses (infantile) sexuality exclusively in terms of non-functional bodily pleasures. The perversions are nothing but fixations on certain partial drives and to specific erogenous zones. They originate in an excess of pleasure . . . and nothing allows us to explain heterosexuality differently.[1]

The later editions, however, have given rise to more conservative positions with regard to the same topic. In these later editions the perversions are interpreted as developmental disorders and, more generally, as pathological deviations. In Freud's later work, more concretely, perversion is considered to be a defence against the traumatic confrontation with sexual difference. This idea became the standard psychoanalytic theory of perversion from Stoller (Stoller 1975) to Lacan. As a result, heterosexuality risks being regarded as the 'normal' outcome of psychosexual development. This explains, at least in part, the conservative and sometimes violent reactions in some psychoanalytic circles in France occasioned by the parliamentary discussions about same-sex marriage and adoption.

In the first edition of the *Three Essays*, Freud identifies sexuality with non-functional bodily pleasures. In this text sexuality is conceptualized without any reference to sexual difference. This approach allows Freud to conceive of the different sexual orientations as *mere* variations, thus preventing them from being in one way or another (morally) rejected. But Freud did not develop this approach any further in his later work. Quite the contrary. In his texts on fetishism, he looks for a specific mechanism that distinguishes perversion from the other pathologies. Perversion is now thought of as a specific defence against the traumatic confrontation with sexual difference. Heterosexuality tends to be seen as the 'normal' outcome of psychosexual development again . . . from a 'poetic fable' it becomes once again the desired outcome of a complex we know as psychoanalysis's shibboleth (Van Haute 2002).

All of this implies that the *Three Essays* cannot be read as unambiguous answers to clearly formulated questions. On the contrary, these essays illustrate the complex problematic that we inherit from Freudian psychoanalysis. They teach us above all that psychoanalysis is not an answer, but a field of related questions and problematics. This book tried to show that these questions can and should be kept alive by situating Freud in his historical context. At the same time, it confronts Freud both with his own ambiguities and inconsistencies (or – if one prefers – paradoxes) and the solutions that the psychoanalytic tradition gave to them. Should sexuality be understood from the perspective of its object or not? Can we thematize sexuality without a reference to the (oedipal?) law and what are the consequences of such a thematization? What is the relation between human sexual constitution and the cultural formation of morality and intellectual life? Does sexuality find its origin in the Other or is it determined by internal factors? What is the status of the perversions and what do they teach us about the relation between 'normality' and pathology in the field of sexuality? These questions that Freud's *Three Essays* have bequeathed us remain urgent for contemporary debates inside and outside of psychoanalysis.

Note

1 This implies that these fixations have no defensive meaning as they have in later texts. We will come back to this problem in the next paragraph.

References

Davidson, A.I. (2001). *The Emergence of Sexuality: Historical Epistemology and the Formation of Concepts.* Cambridge, MA: Harvard University Press.

Jung, C.G. (1907). *Über die Psychologie der Dementia Praecox.* Halle: Verlagsbuchhandlung Carl Marhold.

Micale, M. (1993). On the "Disappearance" of Hysteria. A Study in the Clinical Deconstruction of a Diagnosis. *Isis* 84, 496–526.

Stoller, R. (1975). *Perversion: The Erotic Form of Hatred.* New York: Pantheon.

Van Haute, P. (2002). The Introduction of the Oedipus Complex and the Re-Invention of Instinct. *Radical Philosophy* 115, 7–15.

INDEX

'accidental factors' 94–6
activity and constraint 93–4
affectivity 57
aggression 24, 36, 65, 73–5; *see also* masochism; sadism
aim, sexual 9, 33–4, 71–2, 80, 90, 93
algolagnia 64, 73–4
anaesthesia 66
anxiety 88–9, 96, 108
autoerotism 12–15, 36–8, 57, 105

bisexuality 35, 48; theory of original 68–70, 76–7; *see also* inversion
Bleuler, Eugen 29, 39–40, 56, 57
body, the 87–90, 97–8
Body and Language in Psychoanalysis (David-Ménard) 89–90, 96
Boiste, Pierre 64
bondage 68, 75
breast: child's attachment to 18; sucking of 13–15, 37
Butler, Judith 96–8

cannibalistic theory 67, 70, 74–5
castration, law of 107–9
clinical vs conceptual perspectives 87
conflict, human 19–20
contrectation 81
conversion hysteria 77–8
cruelty 69, 81–4; *see also* sadism
cultural context 52–3
cultural conventions 33–4, 39

Darstellung 89–90
Davidson, A. 103–6
death instinct 94–6
degeneration 44, 49, 66–8, 72
destiny 92
disgust 33–5, 73, 77
drive(s): 'accidental factors' 94–6; displacements of erogeneity 96–8; dualities in concept of 87–90; fundamental 41n4, 55–6; vs instincts 30; loss and 38, 92; partial 31, 91–2, 104–5; sexual 29–31; variability 90–4; *see also* instincts
dualities, breaking with 87–90
Dupré, Ernest 110–13

ego 59–61
emotional charge 56–7
erased sentence in *Three Essays* 55–63
erogeneity, displacements of 89, 96–8
erogenous zones 35, 37, 105
erotogenic zones 14, 78–83, 85n5
evaluation of sexual practices 23–5, 26n10
excremental functions 34, 35, 42n7

fantasy 58, 60–1
father: child's relationship with 19, 35; law of 107–9
females and sadism/masochism 67–8
femininity 48
fetishism 29, 36, 48–9

Foucault, Michel 3–4, 87, 103–4, 112
Freud, Anna 7

gender norms 97–8
genital zone 38, 83, 105–6
Geschlechtstrieb (genital drive) 29, 30; Freud challenges concept 71; procreational norm 65–6; vs *Sexualtrieb* 32
Green, André 22

Heimann, Paula 13–14
hereditary degeneration 44, 49, 66–8, 72
heteronormativity 112; in *Three Essays* 2–3
heterosexuality 32, 48, 118
homosexuality 24, 40, 48, 51–2, 57–60, 61–2; *see also* inversion
hunger 66–7, 71, 74
hyperaesthesia 66
hypochondria 96–7, 98
hysteria: as model for sexuality 34–6; move away from model 39–41, 116; perversions and 70; as research matrix 72–80, 83–5

ideas 97–8
identity 50–1, 103, 106–12, 113n3
impersonal prehistory 19–20, 21
incest barrier 16
infantile sexuality 2–3, 12–14, 32, 36–8, 81–4
ingestion 14, 26n3, 31
instincts: component 55–6, 72, 74, 78–9; vs drives 30; and objects 11–12, 19–20, 33; objects and 6–7; parental love and 16; prehistory of 19–20; reproduction instinct 29; sadism/masochism and 79–84; *see also* drive(s)
Instinkt or *Trieb* 30, 31–2, 41n5
inversion 29, 68, 71, 90

Jung, Carl Gustav 39–40, 56–7, 60–1

kissing 33, 34, 37
Klein, Melanie 7, 13, 17, 25n2, 64
knowledge 96–7
Krafft-Ebing, Richard von: concepts of sadism/masochism (s/m) 64–5; infantile sources of s/m 81–4; modernization of sexuality 47–54; overview of work 44–6; perverse identities 103, 107; perversions, in *Three Essays* 70–1; psychoneuroses and s/m 77–81; sexuality defined 29; s/m as perversions 72–7; s/m in the *Psychopathia Sexualis* 65–70; work elaborated by Freud 72–6, 84–5

Lacan, J.: *Darstellung* and 89–90; Dupré's influence 110–11; Freudian psychoanalysis and 101–2, 111–13; perverse structure and 106–10
lack, law of 107–9
Landauer, Karl 87, 89
language of the body 87–90, 98–9
Laplanche, J. 17–18, 26n5, 26n8
law 112; subversion of 107–9
libido 6–7, 14, 41n2, 48, 51; withdrawal of 56–7, 59–60
loss of object 37–8, 92
Lutschen 37

male sexuality and sadism 67, 73–5
masculinity 48
masochism: concept of 48, 64–5; Freud elaborates Krafft-Ebing's work 72–3, 75–6, 84–5; as perversion 29, 72–3, 75–7; psychoneuroses and 77–81; in *Psychopathia Sexualis* 65–6, 67–70; related to sadism 69–70, 76–7
mastery, drive for 36, 82–4
melancholy 38
metapsychology 64–5, 101–2
modernization and social context 52–3
Moll, Albert: background and work 44–6; modernization of sexuality 47–54; *Trieb* or *Instinkt* 30
morality 52–3, 111–12
mothers 7, 16, 19, 22, 107–8, 113n10

narcissism 24, 40
neuroses and perversions 36, 90–1
neurotic structures 110
normality: Freudian deconstruction 24–5, 111, 117–18; and perversions 67, 71–2; variability in 90–1
normalizing tendencies of psychoanalysis 3, 98–9, 102, 113n1

object-relatedness of sexuality: Freud's contradictory position 13–16, 21–2; making sense of contradictions 16–21; as primary 7–8, 14–15; puberty 38–9; sexuality not object-related 11–13, 22, 104; in *Three Essays* 8–10; turn from hysteria to 39–41, 116–17
objects: aims, reaction formations and 32–4; as basis for study of sexuality 32–3;

choice of 12–13, 117; and instincts 11–12, 19–20, 33; instincts and 6–7; Oedipal relations 15–17, 24; re-finding in puberty 37–8; role of 6–8, 20; value of sexuality 23–5
obsessional neurosis 36, 40–1, 80, 117
Oedipus complex: evolution of Freud's theory 2–4, 17–19; lacking in *Three Essays* 17; model of hysteria and 35–6; object relations 7–8, 15–17, 24; obsessional neurosis and 41; psychoanalysis and 15–16
orality 81–2
organ-pleasure 91–2
Other, the 96, 107–8, 111, 112
overvaluation 75, 91

pain 68, 69, 73, 98
paradoxia 66
paraesthesia 66
parent-child relationships 15–16; *see also* Oedipus complex
patho-analysis 101–2, 106–7
perverse structures 102, 106–11
perverse subjects 107–9, 111–12, 114n14
perversions: anthropology of 101–2; building blocks of sexuality 31, 72, 104–5; classification of 47–9, 66; definitions 23–4, 30, 72; as evidence for theory of sexuality 32–3; Freudian views 23–4; as functional signs of degeneration 66; Krafft-Ebing, sadism and masochism 73–81; Lacan's rethinking of 106–10; neuroses and 34–6; normality and 67, 71–2; origins of 103; relational dimensions and 52
perversities 67, 107
'perverts' 103–6, 109
phallic experience 97–8
phantasy 49, 61, 66, 68, 76, 77
phylogenesis 57, 60–1
pity 83–4
plasticity of the drive 88, 93–4, 98
pleasure 35, 51–2, 73, 105, 112
Pontalis, J.B. 17–18, 26n5
pressure 93–4, 95
procreative norm, move away from 48, 51–2, 104
propagation 29, 61
psychiatry and Freud: on autoerotism 36–8; Freud's discussion with psychiatry 28–32; hysteria as model for sexuality 34–6; influence of French psychiatry 110–11; on puberty 38–9; on sexual objects, aims and reaction formations 32–4; shift from hysteria to object 39–41, 116–17

psychic, the 88–9
psychoanalysis: conceptual framework 30–2; cultural norms and 101; developed through *Three Essays* 28; Oedipus complex and 15–16; opposing world views and 21–2; risk of becoming normalizing 3, 98–9, 102, 113n1; sexuality and 118
psychology: individual and social 7–8; and understanding of sexuality 49–50, 52–3
psychoneuroses 77–81
Psychopathia Sexualis 65–70, 103
psychoses 39–40, 116–17
psychotic process 56–7
puberty 13, 14, 37–9

reaction formations 32–4, 111
relational dimension of sexuality 21, 51–2
religion 57–8, 60–2
reproduction instinct 29

Sade, D.A.F. de 64, 106, 108
sadism: characteristics of 68–9; Freud elaborates Krafft-Ebing's work 72–5, 84–5; Lacan's approach 106; as perversion 29, 72–7; psychoneuroses and 77–81; in *Psychopathia Sexualis* 65–70; related to masochism 69–70, 76–9; terminology 64; in *Three Essays* 64–5
Schiller, Friedrich von 65
schizophrenia 62
Schreber case 57–60, 61–2
scopophilia 80–1, 83
seduction theories 17–18, 35–6, 42n8
self-preservation 31, 67
sexual aims 9, 33–4, 71–2, 80, 90, 93
sexual bondage 68, 75
sexual difference 38–9, 112, 118
sexual objects *see* objects
sexual orientation 48, 52, 118
sexuality: definition 23–5; developmental approach 40, 59, 117–18; difference and 112; Freud's challenges to functional approach 71, 104, 117; functional approach 29, 32, 103; as natural force 47; object-relatedness 11–13, 20–2; pre-Freudian understanding 28–30, 44; psychological understanding of 49–50; relational dimensions 21, 51–2; social context of 52–3; theories of 32–3; in *Three Essays* 9–10
Sexualtrieb vs *Geschlechtstrieb* 32
shame 33, 73, 77
skin 80–1

society: as context 52–3; and perversions 109, 112
somatic, the 88–9
structures 106–9
sub-cultures 51
submission 67–9
sucking 13–15, 31, 37, 81–2

Three Essays on the Theory of Sexuality: contemporary relevance 8–9, 21–2, 25, 118–19; in context 28–9, 116; contradictions within 16–19, 25; erased sentence 55–63; tone 9–10, 21; versions 1–5, 28, 102, 104, 118
thumb sucking 14
trauma theory 34–6
Trieb or *Instinkt* 30, 31–2, 41n5

variability of drive components 90–4
variation, need for 33
Verhaeghe, P. 106–7, 110
violence 69; *see also* sadism

Taylor & Francis eBooks

Helping you to choose the right eBooks for your Library

Add Routledge titles to your library's digital collection today. Taylor and Francis ebooks contains over 50,000 titles in the Humanities, Social Sciences, Behavioural Sciences, Built Environment and Law.

Choose from a range of subject packages or create your own!

Benefits for you
- Free MARC records
- COUNTER-compliant usage statistics
- Flexible purchase and pricing options
- All titles DRM-free.

Benefits for your user
- Off-site, anytime access via Athens or referring URL
- Print or copy pages or chapters
- Full content search
- Bookmark, highlight and annotate text
- Access to thousands of pages of quality research at the click of a button.

REQUEST YOUR FREE INSTITUTIONAL TRIAL TODAY

Free Trials Available
We offer free trials to qualifying academic, corporate and government customers.

eCollections – Choose from over 30 subject eCollections, including:

Archaeology	Language Learning
Architecture	Law
Asian Studies	Literature
Business & Management	Media & Communication
Classical Studies	Middle East Studies
Construction	Music
Creative & Media Arts	Philosophy
Criminology & Criminal Justice	Planning
Economics	Politics
Education	Psychology & Mental Health
Energy	Religion
Engineering	Security
English Language & Linguistics	Social Work
Environment & Sustainability	Sociology
Geography	Sport
Health Studies	Theatre & Performance
History	Tourism, Hospitality & Events

For more information, pricing enquiries or to order a free trial, please contact your local sales team:
www.tandfebooks.com/page/sales

 Routledge
Taylor & Francis Group

The home of Routledge books

www.tandfebooks.com